P9-CQP-498

ON POWER

ALSO BY GENE SIMMONS

ON POWER

MY JOURNEY THROUGH THE CORRIDORS OF POWER

AND HOW YOU CAN GET
MORE POWER

GENE SIMMONS

HarperCollins books may be purchased for educational, business,
or sales promotional use. For information please e-mail the Special
Markets Department at Spsales@harpercollins.com.

FIRST EDITION

Designed by Michelle Crowe

Library of Congress Cataloging-in-Publication Data has been applied for.

ISBN 978-0-06-269470-6 (hardcover)
ISBN 978-0-06-283682-3 (B&N BF Signed Edition)
ISBN 978-0-06-284226-8 (B&N Signed Edition)

17 18 19 20 21 DIX/LSC 10 9 8 7 6 5 4 3 2 1

To my mother, Florence,
who taught me to reach for the stars.
To Shannon, Sophie, and Nick,
for making me a better man, a devoted father,
husband . . . and piñata.
And finally, to you, who remind me
that I wasn't born me.
I had to create me. And you can create you.

CONTENTS

WHO AM I?

It's a valid question. If you've read anything else I've put out into the world, you may think you know my story. Lord knows I love talking about myself. But if you've heard it before, you need to hear it again, this time in a new context. In this book, I'm going to tell you the story of how *I achieved power*. And I'm going to tell you how you can do the same. You too can be powerful. So strap in and prepare for the ride.

I'm Gene Simmons. You know, that weird guy who always sticks his tongue out. I cofounded KISS, America's #1 gold-record-award-winning group of all time in all categories. In some circles, I'm kind of a big deal. And I recognize and understand that, humbleness be damned.

But I wasn't born Gene Simmons. That's not even my birth name. I created Gene Simmons. I gave myself that name. My name is part of the destiny that I created for myself. Similarly, a prime minister isn't born the prime minister. The president isn't born the president. A CEO isn't born a CEO. The pope isn't even born the pope. Powerful people attain power by making certain choices and by possessing the desire to be something bigger. Granted, it also takes a lot of luck and being in the right place at the right time. There are many factors that you can't control—your background, your place in history, your environment—and these things will either help you or hold you back. But they are your circumstances, not your destiny. And you have no choice but to roll with them. In the end, it is up to you to make your own destiny. It is up to you to enter the ring with your fists up. And to train. Hard.

So who am I, really?

I was born in Haifa, Israel, on August 25, 1949. This was a tumultuous time in the world. People were still recovering from World War II, the war that was supposed to end all wars. More than sixty million people had been killed, and millions more were seriously injured. My own mother, Florá, was a victim of the war, by virtue of the fact that she was Jewish. Her family was from Hungary, and when she was just fourteen years of age, they were all shipped off to the concentration camps in Nazi Germany. Two of her brothers had escaped to America right before the war, but of the family members who had remained in Europe, only my mother survived.

After the war, my mother immigrated to the newly formed State of Israel, which became an independent country on May 14, 1948. She met teacher and carpenter Yechiel Witz, and they married. I was born a year later. As a child I was unaware that there was constant conflict with neighboring states that didn't want Israel to exist. At age four, I didn't understand why my father had to dress up in a uniform and go out to the road, machine gun in hand, to hitch a ride for what I later learned were the front lines. Israel is such a small country that you could literally get into a taxi, or hitch a ride, and be at the front lines of a war zone within an hour or two. My childhood was happy, as I remember it. Once I got older I would learn how difficult those early years were for my family. But as a child I did not know what I was missing.

We didn't own a television; I had never seen or heard of TV. We didn't have a bathroom; we had to go to the outhouse. I had never heard of Kleenex or tissues or the idea that you could use something *once* and then throw it away. We didn't even have toilet paper. We used rags that my mother would cut from a larger piece of cloth we no longer used. Those rags were used to blow our noses, to clean things, and, yes, to wipe our behinds. And then my mother would wash those rags and reuse them, again and again. She never threw anything away. And maybe that explains why, to this day, I will wear a shirt or a pair of jeans until it tears and falls off me.

By the time I was old enough to start going to public school in Israel, my father had left us. I didn't understand it at the time, but my mother was with me and, it seemed, she was all I needed.

One day, we received a CARE Package. CARE (Cooperative for American Relief Everywhere) was an organization that sent food and goods to people in underdeveloped countries. To my knowledge, we had never received mail of any kind, much less a big box addressed to my mother. We tore open the box, and inside, we found things I had never seen before. There was a sweater. It was too big for me, but nonetheless I wore it every day, proudly. It had holes in it, and my mother would occasionally sew the holes back up. There was also a big can of peaches. I had never seen or heard of peaches. In Israel, we had cactus fruit that grew on the hill behind our small one-bedroom home, which was riddled with scars from artillery fire from neighboring countries. We didn't have a can opener, so my mother used a big rock to punch a hole on one side of the can. Once she'd opened the can, she offered me a swig of nectar. To this day, I vividly recall it as the sweetest taste I had ever experienced. It was thick and seemingly unnatural. Fruit didn't taste like that. And neither did cake, the few times we'd had any. And perhaps my first experience with that can of peaches explains why I have an insatiable sweet tooth to this day.

There was also a Bugs Bunny book, where Elmer Fudd was constantly chasing the rabbit. I had never heard of Bugs and didn't recall much of the book until we immigrated to America and I started seeing Bugs Bunny cartoons on television. Because my mother couldn't read or speak English at the time, she would just look at the pictures in the book and tell me a story as if she were reading from those pages. On many nights, I would sometimes wonder why the story in the book kept changing. There were other wonders in that CARE Package too. I'll never forget it. Somewhere out there was a kind, anonymous stranger who'd sent the box to us.

My takeaway from that experience is that we all must give back. We *must*. My story and my mother's story are not the only tales of heartache and poverty. It continues today. So much of the world trudges on, in the same conditions or worse, as wars are being fought for nothing. Because of hatred, racism, and tribalism. And children continue to go to sleep hungry. And that's partly why I've always been so driven. I've always wanted power, but not so much for myself or for attaining material wealth. (I don't have much use for material things. I simply don't shop. I can't. I start to sweat when someone comes up to me in a store and asks me if I want help. I can't even order a coffee at Starbucks.) Instead, power for me is about the ability to fulfill your dreams, to support your family, and, most important, to give back, whether it's through using my success to create jobs or my celebrity to bring awareness to a good cause.

The charities I'm involved with are incredibly important to me: Mending Kids, which sends doctors around the world to perform free operations on children who would otherwise be doomed to a life of pain or death; the Shriners Hospitals for Children, the charitable branch of the Shriners organization that performs operations on children in America free of charge; the Pediatric AIDS Foundation, which is devoted to preventing pediatric HIV and eliminating pediatric AIDS; Matter, which sends shiploads of medicine, canned goods, and more to areas of the world in need; the Starkey Hearing Foundation, which sends free hearing aids to families around the world; and, of course, the Wounded Warrior Project, which supports our vets.

Why do I give back? Because I believe that we should all try to make this world a better place than when we came into it. That's my motivation for giving back. What's yours? Maybe it's that you want your mother to be proud of you. Maybe you want God to give you the thumbs-up for being a good person. But really, you should be doing it for yourself. Because you could just as easily have been born in a Third World country, watching your child go to sleep hungry each night, or worse. I'm aware that this isn't the sort of language I use in my pop culture job. But this is where I get to clear the air and bare my soul. For you. For me.

When I was eight years old, my mother told me that we were going on a trip, and I was excited, to say the least. We took the bus from our home in Tirat Ha-Carmel to Haifa, and I found myself standing next to my mother in a large office, at the end of a long line of people. Ahead of us stood a uniformed man behind a big desk, in front of a multicolored flag I had never seen before. The flag was red, white, and blue, with a field of stars in the corner. And surprisingly, the man in uniform motioned for us to move forward, so we walked to the front of the line. He began asking my mother questions in broken Hebrew, but it was clear to me that the uniformed man and my mother couldn't fully understand each other. (At home we spoke Hebrew and Hungarian, my mother's native language. I also knew some Turkish and Spanish, and my mother had learned German in order to survive in Nazi Germany.) He asked her if she spoke English. The answer was no. He asked her if she spoke other languages. And sadly, my mother had to admit that she spoke German well enough, despite the pain it caused her to recall it. The uniformed man asked her some questions in German and my mother answered them.

What happened next, I will never forget as long as I live. The uniformed man asked my mother to raise her hand to swear allegiance to America. And because my mother had never before sworn an oath in this way, she was confused, and she raised her entire arm . . . in a Nazi salute. I suppose that must have been the image she'd seen in her younger years in the concentration camps. And that blessed man quickly came around from behind the desk over to where we were standing and pushed my mother's arm down to her side.

He smiled at us and said, "You will never have to do that ever again. You're going to America." And my mother cried. She still does at the mere mention of the experience.

In the summer of 1958, we arrived in New York and moved in temporarily with her brother Larry in Brooklyn (one of the two brothers who had escaped before the war). Soon thereafter, my mother started working in a sweatshop, earning half a cent for every button she could sew on to winter coats. She was lucky to clear $100 per week, working six days a week, from seven in the morning until seven at night. When my mother would come home at night she would collapse and watch TV with me. Before we went to sleep, we would watch something called "High Flight," which was shown on TV stations at the time as a sign-off at the end of the broadcast day (search for it on YouTube). I remember it as if it were yesterday: a U.S. Air Force jet would streak through the heavens, and a man's voice would recite a poem about flying with patriotic music in the background. The poem ends with: "Put out my hand and touched the face of God." And then the television would slowly fade to static. Once the TV was off, I'd look up at my mother's face and realize how hard she'd been crying. I wondered for years why my mother would cry when she saw the American flag. And eventually it dawned on me: she had seen so much misery, pain, and death in her life, and finally, she was in a country that allowed her to breathe free. And feel safe.

Now that I'm older, I understand. When I see the American flag going up a flagpole, I often find myself with tears falling down my face. Perhaps this story helps you to understand why people of my generation, especially immigrants, say corny things like "God bless America" and mean it.

God bless America, indeed.

By the fall of 1958, my mother enrolled me in yeshiva, a Jewish theological seminary. I was there six days a week, studying from 7:00 A.M. until 9:30 P.M.

Half the day was spent on studying the Talmud and Torah. The other half was dedicated to history, math, and so on. Once I got home from school, there wasn't time for much else, other than watching a bit of TV before bed. And strangely, TV turned out to be my greatest early influence. I desperately wanted to learn all that I could about America. Its history. Its people. Its culture. I wanted to be American. And TV helped me to understand America. The language. The food. And the astonishing opulence. Everything was new to me—and exciting. It seemed that there were no limits. I saw cowboys from the 1800s. I saw monster movies. I saw a man with a cape flying through the air. And then I discovered comic books. Superman and Batman were mythological in what they could accomplish. I was hooked on all things American. My imagination soared, and every day I envisioned myself as a cowboy or Superman.

By 1960, a full year and a half after we first arrived in America, I was still known as Haim Witz and spoke English with a thick accent. Then I decided to change my name to Gene Klein. Klein was my mother's maiden name, and I'm not sure where Gene came from. Perhaps it was from watching one of my favorite TV westerns, *Bat Masterson,* starring Gene Barry. I also began to notice that the people in my neighborhood (Williamsburg, Brooklyn) didn't sound like the newscasters on television, and the people walking the streets with me didn't dress as well as them either. So as I was learning to speak English, I mimicked TV anchormen and thereby avoided the various New York accents.

I didn't know it at the time, but I was making decisions that would create a marketable product. And that product was *me*.

I took steps to *rebrand* myself, beginning with changing my name to sound more American. I worked hard to get rid of my accent. And yes, I took off my yarmulke (the skull cap that Jews of certain beliefs often wear). While I know that every race and creed has pride in its own unique culture, the *real world works differently*. Everyone is proud of his own culture, but we should communicate in a common language and uphold certain cultural/economic/political ideals. Maybe we don't have to build a Tower of Babel to challenge God in heaven, but it sure would be a good idea if we could all communicate with one another. And in America, that means speaking English, regardless of our birth language.

Take a cue from the airline industry. Recently, when I flew on Singapore Airlines to Beijing, where they speak Mandarin, I noticed that the proud Singaporean pilots and the proud Chinese airport officials all communicated in English. Why? Because the airline industry has a *business to run*. It will use whatever language gets it the most money. English has become the common language, the lingua franca, and speaking English has become essential for communication, more important than waving your own flag/culture/language in other people's faces. And that's a good lesson for you. And me.

Here's the truth: You will be judged by others, whether you like it or whether it's fair. Every day, wherever you go. You will be judged by how you look. How you speak. How you present yourself. It's not socially acceptable to say certain things publicly, and perhaps rightfully so. But privately, people are thinking all sorts of things. The law can't control our thoughts (at least not yet). And it's up to you to be the best version of *you*. Or not. You are also free to be who you want to be, without making any compromises, and the rest of the world be damned.

But if you want success—and I wanted success—you have to play by certain rules. For me, that meant playing by *their* rules. Not mine. And that's because *they* owned the world. And *they* had the power. And *they* had the money and everything else that I wanted. In return for making some personal adjustments and rebranding myself, I saw that *they* would give me everything I wanted. And I thought that was more than a fair deal. When I finally ruled the world, I could make the changes I wanted. But raging against the world when you have no power does not accomplish much.

When in Rome, do as the Romans do.

Dress British, think Yiddish.

Early on, these notions were very clear in my head, because I was so grateful to be in this new place called America. And then I discovered that the radio played a kind of music I had never heard before, and it hooked me: rock and roll. Chuck Berry, Little Richard, and Elvis Presley. It must have struck my mother as odd to hear her son singing words in English that he didn't fully understand, in his thick Israeli accent. And I tried to move like those guys. I shook my hips. When Chubby

Checker hit it big with "The Twist" (both a song and a popular dance at the time), I was intent on becoming the best twister of them all. And I was, at least locally. At the seventh grade dance, I won the twist contest with an African American girl in my class named Shirley. Together, we knew how to *do it to it,* as they used to say. My prize? A Nat King Cole 45 rpm record. In those days, a vinyl 45 rpm single consisted of a song on one side and the B song on the other side.

I was starting to think about money and girls, and I wanted both. I started working at all sorts of odd jobs after school and on weekends. I delivered newspapers door-to-door. I probably made $15 per week on my newspaper route, and by the end of the year, I had saved about $600. I had never seen so much money. Then another kid in the neighborhood who also had a paper route decided that he'd rather go to the playground and play softball than deliver papers, so I took over his route in addition to mine. I also worked at a butcher's shop, scrubbing the fat and drying blood off the chopping block daily. I also brought up big pieces of meat from the rat-infested storage area in the basement. Eventually, I was clearing about $25 per week, times fifty weeks, and had saved about $1,000 (a lot back then).

And then in 1964, at age fourteen, I witnessed the Beatles. And I had a vision. Things all started to make sense. I wanted to be in a band. To make money. To get girls. To be accepted. This was the beginning of a phase in my life I like to call A.B. (After the Beatles), when I was in various bands, which we'll get to later. But

I didn't quit my day job, as the saying goes. I continued working and saving money. I continued to do well in school. And I stayed away from smoking, drinking, and, later, doing drugs. Everyone seemed to be indulging in these things in the sixties, but they simply had no appeal for me. They still don't. I couldn't imagine disappointing my mother after the hard life she had led. She'd fought so hard to keep me safe. How could I endanger myself or embarrass her after all that? I promised myself that I would succeed and make my mother's life easier. I didn't want her to work. I wanted to buy her a house. I wanted to give her all the things she'd never had. I was intent on making all of this happen.

In high school, I was drawn to Junior Achievement, an activity where local captains of industry took the time to teach teenagers about how capitalism works. The things I learned in Junior Achievement have served me well to this day. I would urge you to get the young people in your life into Junior Achievement or the equivalent in your community. Unfortunately, the school system doesn't teach kids what a mortgage is or how taxes and businesses work. While students learn basic mathematics and various historical facts, very little of what they learn in school equips them with the practical tools they'll need to enter adulthood and the workforce. Junior Achievement taught me how a business works, from raising capital, to selling shares of stock, to marketing a product, buying insurance, and hoping to see a profit after all costs. Oh yes, and then there are the corporate and personal taxes on profits. Young people need to go through this sort of training to prepare for the real world. Knowing that Columbus discovered America in 1492 (which is, of course, incorrect; he discovered nothing since Indians had been here for more than twelve thousand years) will mean nothing when you go out for your first job.

After school hours, when I wasn't attending Junior Achievement classes down at the YMCA, I would hit the library and voraciously devour books—all kinds of books. I was also in the acting society (Masque & Bauble) and the school choir. And then I noticed that all the girls were registered in the typing class, so I enrolled. I learned to type very fast (close to 100 words per minute), and I also got a few dates in there. Little did I know that my typing abilities would eventually open doors for me.

After high school, I understood that the next step was to go to college. So I took out a loan and enrolled in a community college in upstate New York, eventually graduating with a bachelor of arts in education. While I was in college, I also played with a rock band, worked as a floor manager in a warehouse and as a lifeguard at the Pines Hotel, and had my own typing service where students paid me fifty cents for every double-spaced page I typed up. All at the same time. Once I graduated with my degree, I was hired by a temp agency called Kelly Girl Service (eventually changed to Kelly Services), a company that major corporations turned to when they needed additional manpower. My typing skills got me in, and that opened the door to working a temp job at a legal firm called Williamson & Williamson on Wall Street—the night shift—from

8:00 P.M. till 7:00 A.M. Then I was hired for a temp position at *Glamour* magazine and in short order was offered a spot at *Vogue,* where I found myself working for a time as man Friday to the iconic managing editor of the magazine, Kate Lloyd.

In my twenties, I was always employed. Hard work was in my DNA, ingrained from the time I was a boy, seeing my mother get up at the crack of dawn every day to go to work. After *Vogue,* I got a job as assistant to the director of the Puerto Rican Interagency Council (a government-funded research and demonstration project). After work, I'd go to my second job as a check-out guy at a New York City deli. Then, for a short stint, I actually put my education degree to use and taught sixth grade in Spanish Harlem.

At this point, the year was 1973 and I had just turned twenty-three. I was in New York City, in the right place at the right time, and then I found the right thing: KISS. In the next chapter, I'll tell you more about exactly how KISS started. But for now I want you to focus on the fact that in the early years of KISS, I was still living at my mother's house, because I wanted to save on rent, and I didn't care what anyone had to say about that.

I also did not own a car until I turned thirty-four.

I hardly bought anything. I simply didn't need *things*. I had no interest in clothing or gadgets.

Keep It Simple, Stupid (KISS).

I had also amassed $23,000, after taxes, which meant I had actually earned and saved quite a bit more. I was almost there.

Let me also take a moment to tell you about some decisions I made about my personal life at the time. This may not endear me to some readers, but let's be honest: there is little that a young man has to offer when he is just starting out on his journey. He hasn't yet made his fortune. He is ill equipped to settle down—and that's being kind. Ladies, you may think that the six-foot-tall guy you are looking at is a man, but if he is between twenty and thirty years of age, what you're really seeing is a fourteen-year-old trapped in a man's body whose decisions are being dictated by his testosterone. In other words, he's not ready for a relationship—no steady girlfriend, no marriage. It's not his fault. It's just the way he's built. I recognized this about myself, and when I was in my twenties, I decided that I didn't want a serious relationship. I didn't want anything or anyone to get in the way of my dreams.

The fact is that everything and everyone in your life takes time, effort, and money, in some sense. When you are romantically involved with someone, you have to spend time and money on him or her. When I was young, I had as much company as I wanted, but I didn't let that take time away from my devotion to *myself*. My dreams. My aspirations. I talked a lot about this in my previous book *Me, Inc.* But it bears repeating. Shakespeare said, "To thine own self be true," but I recommend going much further. Devote everything you have in your early years to yourself. Don't take vacations. Save all that you can. Work hard. All the time. You'll thank me later.

So there I was, with my money saved, committed

to achieving my dreams. All that was left was the final step in my transformation. In 1973, I was still Gene Klein, but that name simply doesn't work when you're a member of a rock band. I'm not going to spend time lecturing you on what's "cool." But I will say that when you see successful pop culture figures, whether actors, entertainers, or musicians, you notice that they're a bit different from the rest of us, and they have different-sounding names. Can you imagine a proud mother and father looking down at their new baby and saying, "I know what we're going to call our child . . . the Edge." Or Sting. Or Bono. Or Gaga. It doesn't happen. Our parents want the best for us, but this is not the way that they are thinking when we are first born. So it's up to you to create yourself. You like your name? Keep it. But that doesn't mean the rest of us will like it. You like the way you look? Terrific. But that doesn't mean the rest of us will. And so on.

You *can* reinvent yourself—*if* you have the desire.

And I did. I decided I would name myself Gene Simmons.

Just like that.

There are many things in life that you can't control. You're born a certain race, to a certain family and background, for example. And you've got no say in those things. But many other things in life are conscious choices: What name do you want to call yourself? What religion would you like to practice? Where do you want to live? What career do you want to pursue? You can even change your gender, if you like and if you have the funds for the procedure. When it comes to your birth name, don't kid yourself. Your name has *never really been yours*. You had nothing to do with it. Your parents chose it for you, probably before you were born. Or maybe right there on the spot, as you were being born. And if it's not working for you, you can change it.

In America, the bastion of free thought and free choice, you can be anything you want to be. And every choice you make for and about yourself will either give you more power (and therefore money) or less. *Even the name I chose for myself was chosen specifically to achieve power.* This is how much I care about power, and this is how much, I argue, that you should care about it as well.

That is who I am.

If you want to become like me, read on.

A BRIEF KISSTORY

As I've mentioned, when I was fourteen, I first saw the Beatles on *The Ed Sullivan Show*. And while watching, I had what is commonly referred to as a "spiritual experience." In 1964, the population of the United States was about 191.9 million, and a good chunk of the American population—73 million men, women, and children—were also watching. Overnight, all anyone in America could talk about, or think about, was the Beatles. An event like this doesn't happen often, and a band like the Beatles may never happen again.

Their performance affected me in ways I wouldn't understand until years later. Being from another country and a different culture, I wanted desperately to fit in. I felt like an outsider. I still do, I suppose. But right there, in plain sight, were four guys with funny haircuts who clearly didn't look, walk, talk, or sound American. At the time, I remember thinking they looked a little feminine, smaller than most Americans, with finer, gentler features. And since they all had the same mop-top haircut and outfits, they looked like they all came from the same Beatle mother. And right then and there, the Beatles validated for me the idea that you could be different and still be accepted. I saw the entire audience screaming at the top of their lungs. I particularly noticed girls in droves, who were going out of their minds for these guys. And I thought, for the first time, perhaps I should be doing this. Perhaps I should put my weirdness onstage, get a band together, and try to be the Beatles.

I clearly recall dreaming about the idea. I dreamed I was the fifth Beatle. I'm sure others had that fantasy as well. In my dream, I remember walking down to Thirty-Fourth Avenue and Eighty-Second Street in Jackson Heights, Queens (where we were living at the time), with my Beatles haircut and the other guys in the band, on the way to the elevated subway. We walked right by the record store where I'd first bought Chubby Checker's *Twistin' Round the World* record. And then girls started chasing us. We quickly ran up the stairs to the subway platform, bought train tokens, and hopped on the train.

The difference between dreamers (we all dream, after all) and doers is—you guessed it—some of us actually *do* something about it. And I did. In short order,

I put together a band with my schoolmates Seth Dogra-majian and Danny Haber. I named us the Lynx, for some reason. I sang, Seth strummed an acoustic guitar, and Danny played a second guitar and sang harmonies. Beatles songs, Everly Brothers, and so on. We got an of-fer to play a concert in the school cafeteria, and when the school principal introduced us, he said, "Here are the Missing Links." From then on, we were known as the Missing Links.

Other bands quickly followed. The next one I joined was first known as the Long Island Sounds, with band-mates Stephen Coronel, Alan Graf, Stan Singer, and Seth Dogramajian. And then we became the Lovebag (yep, that means exactly what you think it means). We played high school dances and country clubs around Queens, where we all lived. Surprisingly, we made good money, even at our level, and the biggest surprise of all: there were actually more girls interested in us, just because we were onstage. The girls were even interested in yours truly. Time went on. I graduated from college and worked various jobs, and eventually formed a new band called Wicked Lester with Paul Stanley, Brooke Ostrander, Stephen Coronel, and Tony Zarrella. We got an Epic Records deal very fast. But Paul and I literally walked out of our record deal and the band, because we simply didn't believe it could go all the way.

We were in the right place at the right time. But we didn't believe we had the right "thing." So we started all over again and, before long, put a new band to-gether called KISS, with Paul Stanley, Peter Criss, Ace Frehley, and myself. In retrospect, we clearly had no idea what we were doing. The importance of luck and timing is evident here. Sometimes you have to make the leap, even if you don't know what's on the other side. It's not a strategy, per se; it's just a part of life. You cannot know the future. You can only hone your instincts and try to trust them. We had no manager or mentor. But somehow, we seemed to be making the right calls every step of the way.

Paul thought of the name. Ace drew the very first version of our logo, and then Paul redrew the logo with a ruler, to even out the spacing and the lines. And that was the same KISS logo we still use today. Paul and I bankrolled rehearsals, truck rentals, and early band equipment purchases. While I was working as the assistant to the director of the Puerto Rican Interagency Council, I used the office facilities to put together our very first media kit. I wrote the first draft. Paul rewrote some of it. And we took a band photo. All along I had been reading the music trade magazines—*Record World, Billboard, Cash Box*—and I bought every year-end issue and copied down the addresses of every record company and manager listed in the back, making sure all those people got one of our media kits. They say the best way to hit a bull's-eye is to use a machine gun. You'll miss quite a bit. But you will also eventually hit the bull's-eye.

Paul and I booked ourselves a show in the grand ballroom of the Hotel Diplomat in midtown Manhattan. We would always get popular local bands to open for us (though truth be told, they could pull more tickets than we could). I would type up contracts with each group that outlined when they would go onstage and how much they were to be paid. At that grand ballroom show, a band called the Planets opened for us. We were the headliner (though we shouldn't have been), and we were also the promoter and the bank. We grossed about $750, and after all expenses, including paying the Planets $105, we made a profit of a few hundred dollars. By the end of the night, TV producer Bill Aucoin offered to become our manager. Shortly thereafter, Aucoin introduced us to Neil Bogart (former Buddha Records president), who was starting a new label called Casablanca Records. We became the very first band to sign with Casablanca, which would soon become a prominent disco label, representing Donna Summer, the Village People, and many more. But KISS was the first.

We started touring in 1974 in a station wagon, taking turns driving and sleeping in the back. We opened up for headliners who kicked us off tours for getting too many encores. We were on a $75-a-week salary. We wound up in San Francisco completely broke, with just enough money to buy Heinz beans and frozen frankfurters so we could have something to eat. But we kept at it. Day after day. Week after week. And amazingly, it started to work. KISS became so big, in such a short time, that even without a hit single we were headlining Anaheim Stadium in California within a year and a half of signing our record deal. The bands opening for us had been around for at least a decade or more. We started making money. We were shocked to see our licensing and merchandising take off in a big way. We wouldn't let anything or anyone stop us from reaching the top, even when that meant getting rid of problems within the band itself. And the rest, as they say, is history.

For those of you out there reading this, it's worth noting that life choices are important. I won't mince words about it. KISS has made me a rich man. People feel awkward talking about the money they've made, but if someone wins $100 million in the lottery, he has no problem running down the street, announcing the good news to everyone he meets. I, on the other hand, worked every day of my adult life for the money I've made, and I'm proud of it.

Because I worked for it.

And you can do it too.

THE CASE FOR POWER

> It is not surprising that the lambs should bear
> a grudge against the great birds of prey . . . the
> lambs say among themselves, "Those birds
> of prey are evil, and he who is as far removed
> from being a bird of prey . . . is he not good?"
>
> —Friedrich Nietzsche, *The Genealogy of Morals*

You've stuck with me this far, and I thank you. I didn't want to start off the book by lecturing you. But now let's get serious. It's getting late. It's later in your life than you think. But it's never too late to get started.

There is a persistent fallacy in our society, based on an old, musty way of thinking:

Power corrupts.

This idea has worked its way into our cultural narrative in a way few other things have. Watch any children's movie from the past few decades (think rich old

Cruella de Vil or the various "evil" queens from fables and folklore) and you'll know what I mean. It's the same with classics like Charles Dickens's *A Christmas Carol*—you know and hate him: the rich and powerful Scrooge. A pattern emerges, and all of these villains have something in common:

They are rich and powerful.

Often, they are *Machiavellian* in their use of power, a term we'll get into later. But basically, they are relentless, they manipulate to get what they want, and they are ruthless in pursuit of their goals. This trope is found so often in children's stories, and the message we're sending our younger generations is clear:

Bad people are powerful, and being powerful is bad.

So let's not be powerful, then. Let's be meek and timid. Surely everyone will get along better as long as no one gets too powerful. Is this really the lesson above all lessons that we want to teach our children, as we prepare them for what awaits in the real world? I submit to you that it is not. We handicap ourselves by equating power with the villains in fiction.

We do our children a disservice by teaching them to shun power. We deny them the power to seize their dreams. What good is the hero, after all, without the power to defeat the villain? What good could Superman do without his powers? How effective could Batman be without his fortune, his training, his gadgets?

In this book, I intend to make the case for power: what it is, including and beyond money, and why it matters to *everybody*—even the people who claim it "corrupts." So much of our popular mythology focuses on the negative aspects of power that we forget that gaining power is, perhaps, *the only way to enable ourselves to make a difference* in our lives and in the lives of others.

So let's be clear: power is a tool, neither good nor bad. And just because a tool can be abused does not mean that we shouldn't use it. Airlines tell us to secure our own oxygen masks before assisting others, even our children. Why? Is it because selfishness in the face of danger is good? Of course not. It's because this is not a moral argument, but a pragmatic one. We are no good to our children if we can't breathe ourselves. You must be in a *position of power* if you are going to make a difference to those *without power*.

People will rail against greed, against *caring* about power and money. "Some things are more important than money," they say. But what are those things? Being kind to others? Family? Friends? So be it. But our family, our loved ones, the people we want to protect and take care of, all live in the *real* world. And in this real world where we all live, we must *have money* in order to take care of our families. You must first *have money* before you can *give it* to charity. You must have the power and the money to feed your loved ones, to help your friends. And the more money you have, the more you can give, and the better your life and the lives of your loved ones can become. The man who gives away his only dollar is a virtuous soul indeed. But compared with the rich and powerful CEO who gives away $500 million of her $5 billion, he is not making much of a difference, no matter how noble his intentions.

The CEO may be greedier and power-obsessed. Indeed, the CEO might be a grotesque person in her personal life, selfish and vain. But at the end of the day, who fed and clothed more people with their contribution? This is not the romantic ideal we've grown used to. It's not poor, powerless Aladdin defeating rich, evil Jafar. (Incidentally, Aladdin becomes rich by the end of the story, doesn't he?) But this is reality, because in the real world, power matters. Consequences matter, not intentions. A good person without power won't accomplish much, no matter his intentions or his virtue. Power moves mountains, when mountains need to be moved.

The quote at the beginning of this chapter speaks to my point. For those of us who haven't taken Philosophy 101, Friedrich Nietzsche was a German philosopher in the 1800s with a peculiar point of view on the subject of power and its relationship to morality. Often, he was fairly cold and cruel with his criticism, and his unflinching views made a lot of people fairly queasy, and still do. He's been interpreted, criticized, and misinterpreted countless times over the decades. But he also tried to explain the origins of what holds us back from achieving power, what is basically "the worship of weakness." That is the idea that humility and submission are *good,* and that strength, materialism, and ruthlessness are *evil.*

Nietzsche hypothesized that at some point in our history, the weak decided that they disliked the strong and disliked getting the short end of every stick. The old way of dealing with this would have been to find a way to *become* powerful, to improve yourself in order to join the ranks of the strong. Cavemen, Vikings, all our big, muscly warrior ancestors throughout early history shared this ambition. The heroes of old were not saints and charitable souls; they were Beowulf, Heracles, Gilgamesh. However, Nietzsche mused, the weak found another way to ease their own suffering: they made it *unacceptable, undesirable,* to be among the strong. They wanted to make the strong feel *shame* for enjoying their power.

The Bible says, "It is easier for a camel to go through the eye of a needle, than for a rich man to enter the kingdom of God" (Matthew 19:24). Just because he's rich. Nietzsche viewed ideas like this as a sort of mental and cultural coup: the weak persuading the strong to be ashamed of their strength, thus inverting the power dynamic for centuries to come. Instead of raising themselves up to *become* powerful, they shamed those with power into purposefully lowering themselves. They shamed power itself. This, in my view, was throwing the baby out with the bathwater.

Now, it is of course possible for a tyrant to take his power and run with it, and abuse it. Power can be abused by anyone: good, evil, and (like most of us) somewhere in between. But that's not what I'm talking about. We forget that Nietzsche's arguments are by definition amoral: he himself did not believe there were such things as "moral facts." He was simply trying to describe the world as he saw it. This book will similarly be useful to anyone who withholds moral judgment, because it is not about morality. It is about pragmatism and overcoming flawed narratives that hold us back.

People who do great good and people who do great evil have one crucial thing in common: *greatness*. I am not arguing that vile human beings like Hitler are good for humanity. They are not. But the simple fact exists that power is out there for the taking. Why not grab it for the good guys? What keeps the human race evolving so that it can develop ideas like compassion, art, humility, and political correctness? As Nietzsche put it, the main driving force in human society is the "will to power."

Seizing power works.

Being afraid of power, shunning power, stunts your growth.

What gets the job done?

Strength does.

Power does.

This dynamic has been playing out since prehistoric times. The caveman who was strong enough to bring home the most meat got the girl. That is still true today, I might add. The more power and money the male of the species has, the more he has access to in life, and that includes getting the girl. Not politically correct? Of course not. So what? These are concepts from the days before political correctness existed. Nature and reality don't exist to conform to our feelings. Don't like that I cast the caveman as strong and the cavewoman as the weak one waiting for him to bring home dinner? Instead of asking me to conform to your sensitivities, become more powerful than I am and make *your* vision of life dominant. Instead of criticizing those who hold views you find unacceptable, defeat them. Make your own strength and power undeniable. Might does not make right—but might *makes things possible*. It makes things *happen, whether or not they are right*. I argue that this idea, the "will to power," is still just as useful today as it was in prehistory, albeit with less club swinging and mammoth skinning and back hair (though not in my case). However much we might like to pretend that we've moved past Darwin's survival of the fittest, it is still a jungle out there. Fighting to survive, to overcome, to achieve, is still necessary. We must *will* ourselves to power, if we are to earn a place where we have the *luxury* to care about things like compassion, art, and political correctness.

Power is an inconvenient truth, a necessity, whether we like to admit it. To throw a little more philosophy in, it is my opinion (and, really, everything in this book is my opinion) that if you can stand in front of me in clean clothes, knowing how to read, with food in your belly, and say things like, "I don't care about money," or "Power corrupts," you are able to do so only because you are *sheltered*. Frankly, you are *lucky* to be standing on the backs of those with power without realizing it.

In 1943, a psychologist named Abraham Maslow proposed a theory called the Hierarchy of Needs. The basic idea was that *there is an order in which people worry about things* they need to survive and flourish, and he put this in the form of a pyramid. At the base of the pyramid are the "physiological needs," the things that every one of us, from kings to beggars, needs simply to stay alive, things like air, water, food. Without these things, one can only wait until death comes. No one can accomplish anything without these needs being fulfilled. In the world we currently live in, this includes money, because you need money to buy food and to access clean water. Living off the grid is possible, of course, and some people do go out into the woods and try to live off the land. But in this scenario, if your farm fails, if you don't catch any fish, if you fail as a hunter, *you die*. When your basic physical needs are not met, these are the foremost things on your mind. No other concerns can possibly exist when you are starving to death or dying of thirst, and no other goals can be met without first meeting the needs of the flesh.

The next level of Maslow's Hierarchy is "safety." This is where things like shelter, medicine, physical security, and other ways to maintain health and protect from injury reside. Along with money, these things also require a society or system around you that allows you purchase them. That's money and power. Many in the West and especially in European countries argue that health care should be a public, socialized commodity. Whether you agree with this and whether your health care is private or public, power and money are still necessary, to pay for medicine and to fund the health care system. And, of course, there is the prehistoric concept of safety: safety from attack, from predators. This, obviously, requires physical power: the power to defend oneself, to make weapons. In modern society, this means paying your taxes so a police force can be funded and perhaps ponying up for a security system in your home. When you are fed but not safe, it is hard to think of much else. Lost in the woods, in a bad part of town, under attack, or being pursued by a predator—these are all urgent crises that dominate the mind until they are resolved. When you are not safe, safety becomes life's goal until it is met. You are not available to worry about anything else. Once you are fed and safe, you move toward the more familiar stuff that exists in the developed world, what most people reading this book will recognize as their lives.

The next level of the pyramid is "love and belonging." You might call this the need for the *other*: someone to love, sexually or nonsexually; family; friends; a tribe of some kind. A curious thing happens when you reach this level—you can *forget* that this need is *not as important* as the other two. It is my opinion that some people at this level *lack proper perspective*. These are the people who will say things like, "Money is not important, only my [significant other, tribe, or family] is important." This, to me, makes very little sense, since according to the Hierarchy of Needs, money, and the power to acquire things that cost money, is what *allows for the existence of your loved ones*. People who are not starving often feel the need to characterize their lives as a battle between two dueling concepts: "materialistic" concerns and what is "really important" (aka their loved ones). These people forget that there is a lot of money that goes into maintaining a spouse, a family, a tribe.

This, by my interpretation, is where what Nietzsche calls the "inversion of values" has led in the modern era. Instead of thinking of wealth and power as the very means to keep our family alive, we say that these two ideas are mutually exclusive. The dad who works too much is a cliché in many films, especially in holiday movies around Christmastime. I don't think I need to name all of these movies in order for this to sound familiar. (*Elf*, with Will Ferrell, is one of them, but they are countless.) These stories end with the dad learning a valuable lesson and telling his work buddies, or his boss, to shove it: "Instead of doing this very important work, I'm going to spend this time with my family." Throw in some line from the kids like, "We don't need expensive gifts, Papa, we just need you," and the morality tale is complete. This is totally ridiculous. The job in question, and the work it requires, is the most important thing that a father can do for his kids. However, this fact won't be clear until the first two levels in the hierarchy are compromised by something like, for example, a cancer diagnosis. Spending time with the family is a very kind thing for a father to do. But *working through the holidays* so that, when illness strikes, the father has all the resources and power at his disposal to get the best doctors and the best medicine is the better approach, and should be viewed as such. I don't know about you, but I want to make sure the people I love not only feel good and loved, but are *first and foremost* healthy, safe, fed, clothed, and housed. The only reasonable response to "Dad, you work too much" should be "No, I work exactly hard enough to *give you life*."

The next level of Maslow's pyramid is characterized by self-esteem and self-respect. We find the same amnesia here as well. You'll often hear people complain about "working a dead-end job," that their job has nothing to do with their passion and is "just for money." My response to that often is: "Well, *yeah*." Because that money *feeds you*. And yet someone with clothes on their back, a home, and food in their belly will actually complain that their job doesn't engage them, doesn't excite them, or isn't making them *feel good* about themselves. Their boss is *mean* to them when they shirk their responsibilities. The work is *hard*. They feel *inferior* to people who do better than they do, who make more money, who accomplish more. They desire fame, fortune, and success, and ironically some fall into depression and develop inferiority complexes because of these desires. They begin to resent those who are better off, and they resent the system around them that creates their difficulties, their unfair setbacks. People then say the problem is that these people *care about the wrong things,* like money, power, and success. Instead of working *harder* and raising oneself up to achieve these goals, these people fall into self-pity, criticizing those better off as "a-holes," "my awful boss," etc. If you widen this perspective a little by, say, dropping someone off in the middle of a place where they have no access to food, water, and shelter, we would probably find that these concerns disappear almost immediately.

Everything is relative. The person who has no job, no access to income at all, would happily trade places with the person who complains that their boss is "mean" or that they feel "unfulfilled." But most people lack this macro perspective and get caught up in what makes them feel comfortable or uncomfortable in the moment. Instead of self-motivating by dwelling on the power they already possess, how far they've come, and how lucky they are to be fed and safe, they choose to sulk and dwell on how much better off others are. This prevents them from seizing further power for themselves.

The final and highest stage on the pyramid is "self-actualization," which is, essentially, reaching your full potential. Especially in creative industries like writing or music, you'll hear advice like: "Don't do it for money. Don't sell out. Better to be a starving artist." This is another false dichotomy—for art or for money—meaning that the former is goodness and the latter is crass materialism. I've heard this for decades in my industry from many of my peers. They could not comprehend why I would want to do commercials, to sell merchandise, to capitalize on what I helped to create with KISS. "Aren't you selling out?" they would ask. This view is *self-limiting*. It's a *perversion* of what self-actualization actually means, which is the *fulfillment of one's full potential*. Self-actualization is so often looked at as something in *opposition* to the baser needs of the pyramid. But self-actualization cannot be accomplished unless those baser needs have been fulfilled, and fulfilled *many times over*. In layman's terms: *You won't have time to worry about being a good artist if you have no clean water to drink*. You won't have *time* to worry about artistic dignity if you're *dying of hunger*. You'll be too busy worrying about *survival*.

Power is essential for guaranteeing that your most

basic needs will *never* be violated. Worrying about your "artistic integrity" and worrying about being "too materialistic"—these are *luxuries*. These concerns would be absolutely absurd if you didn't first have food, water, shelter, medicine, safety, *and money*. In other words: gaining power, desiring money, and gathering as much of both as you can *has nothing to do with your integrity as an artist*. People who warn you about "selling out" need a *reality check*. Instead of complaining about those with power and wealth selling out, they should focus on improving their own lives. Don't look to see what's on someone else's plate. It's a waste of time. Don't look over your shoulder to see who else is running the race. Just be the best you can be. And then be better.

Worrying about power and money makes you realistic, it makes you a human being with human needs, and it makes you smart. By all means, pursue your dreams, but feed yourself first, and feed your loved ones, lest you forget that you are merely *lucky* to have champagne problems like "selling out" and "artistic anxiety." Please. If you have the opportunity to sell out, that means you've accomplished something. I've said it before, and I'll say it again:

You're damn right I sold out. I sell out every night.

So, now: You want power? You want money? I'm going to try to improve your chances of getting both. Incidentally, one begets the other—the more power you have, the more money you will have, and vice versa.

Power!

Money!

Get used to saying these words. Get rid of that voice in your head that tells you it is wrong to talk about and to go after these things. Our culture tells us we're supposed to keep thoughts about money and power to ourselves. I disagree. Say these words out loud; listen to yourself saying them and pump yourself up. It will embolden you to actually *do* something about your situation, instead of thinking you're a victim. You have to grab life by the scruff of the neck and make the world understand that you are a force to be reckoned with. That you are important. And that you won't accept anything less than the most respectful treatment. You will only get the respect you demand. Take note of those throughout history who demanded respect and saw the results.

When I was in my early teens, the great James Brown released a song called "Say It Loud—I'm Black and I'm Proud!" As a teenager who'd always felt very insecure, it was moving beyond words. Here was a black man who had likely dealt with more struggle in his life than even I had. And he was *loud and proud*. Feeling proud on the inside is one thing. But getting up there and *singing about it publicly,* and *hearing* your own voice saying those words, is something else entirely—it's far more powerful. Until *you* stand up, arch your back, and proclaim to the world and to yourself that you deserve power and everything that comes along with it, until you actually *hear* those words coming out of *your* mouth, they won't fully resonate.

So say it out loud.

Say it out loud to yourself. Every day.

Before a boxer steps into the ring, he has to motivate himself. Before a tightrope walker gets on that wire (especially for the first time), he'd better be telling himself things like, "I know I can do it. I *can* do it." Before a nervous teenager asks a beautiful girl out on a date, he should look in the mirror and *tell himself* that the things he's planning to say will make her heart melt and swoon.

Tell yourself the things that others won't say to you.

You don't need them. *You* should be your own greatest cheerleader and motivator.

If you find yourself at home dipping chips and watching yet another ball game, get up off the couch and say it out loud: "I'm going to *do* something." Sound silly? Well, it works. I talk to myself all the time. I'm doing it right now. It's the only way to get in touch with your true dreams and desires. When I talk to myself and psyche myself up, I tend to actually *do* something as a result. It's certainly more likely than if I'd kept my big piehole shut. Religious motivation is similar. Praying by yourself is all well and good. But how much more motivating is it to go into your place of worship and to hear your pastor/priest/rabbi/etc. preach something, and then to repeat it back?

So, yes, power and money are the essentials. Fame is overrated and fleeting. "Cool" is a moving target and the public is fickle. Power and money are different. If you learn how to harness them, and to use them wisely, they will last you a lifetime. Let's dispel the idea that money and power corrupt and that they are the "root of all evil." Instead, let's embrace the idea that money and power are *the roots that grow all other possibilities in life*. Power has made my dreams come true, provided a wonderful life for my family, and allowed me to be charitable to people I have never met, more so than I ever could have as a poor kid in Israel and then New York.

Power makes *everything* possible.

POWER TOOLS

THE GOLDEN RULE:
He who has the gold makes the rules.

So you've bought this book and you want power. Good. So do I. I always want more power, and you should too. Every day. We'll get into the historical, social, and ethical implications of power a bit later. But first, I want to cut to the chase. Quick and dirty, like a street fight. I want to give you a good, swift kick in the ass, to get your attention and open your eyes to the power that is out there for the taking. And don't stand there waiting for your opponent's jabs to come your way. You need to be the one who strikes first, who moves faster, to take the power away from him.

No one is born powerful. We are all born bald, toothless, and vulnerable. And we're all probably going to die bald, toothless, and vulnerable. But while we're alive . . . we must *live*. When you're a newborn baby, the slightest sound or movement is an assault to your senses. From that point on, gaining power over your environment is a constant uphill battle. It is not easy, and it was never supposed to be easy. Everything from learning to walk to learning how to invest takes immense effort. And, like learning to walk, you will be embarrassed. Your legs will shake. You will fall down. You may even be ridiculed. But then you are going to get back up and do it all over again.

YOU WILL FAIL

Let me be blunt about this fact, and then let me help you. Let me take a pail of ice-cold water and throw it in your face. You must accept this fact of life if you want power. Everything your mother told you about how you are special and how you can succeed at anything you put your mind to is simply not true. You will fail, many times over. Even once you have achieved a modicum of success, you will fail yet again.

But what doesn't kill you makes you stronger. Understanding and embracing this simple truth is what separates the powerful from the weak. This is true, and it will always be true. All the way up to the last breath you take. So ignore the word *no*. And ignore the failure. Every time you step up to the plate and strike out, be ready to push harder and try again. This is the way the world works. I didn't make the rules. I'm just here to remind you that if you choose to believe all the negative crap people throw in your face, *you* will be the architect of your own downfall. Not them. The power is yours.

This is one of the first reviews of KISS, during our very first tour:

SEATTLE DAILY TIMES   May 27, 1974

Music Review

I hope the four guys who make up the group, whose names don't matter, are putting money away for the future. The near future, because **KISS** won't be around long.

This could only be set at

The gentleman who wrote this review of our little band, I am sure, didn't have anything personal against us. I am quite sure he actually believed the words he wrote. So what? We chose to ignore him, as we do all of our critics, and that's why the band is still around and thriving today. Your critics don't count. You must ignore the negatives in your life and continue to move forward. You must be unrelenting and follow your dreams. And you must accept that you will fail. Just like I do. Every day. But I also win. And so will you.

Here's a famous story of failure that may sound familiar to you:

When Harland David Sanders was seven years old, his father came home one day with a fever and later died in his bed, leaving the young boy responsible for feeding his siblings while their mother was at work. It was 1895 and his family had nothing. But he had to find a way to cook for his siblings. So the children all foraged for food, and Sanders learned to cook vegetables and then meat. What started as a bleak tragedy would turn out to be the catalyst for Sanders's calling, despite his absolute lack of power and resources. He eventually left home to work on a farm, and after that he held various jobs until he ended up running a Shell service station in Kentucky. By this time it was the Depression, and Sanders was dead broke. He decided to start selling chicken in his service station as a way to make some extra money.

Sanders was pressed for time, as his customers came to his station for gas, not to eat. The food was an afterthought, and he needed to find a way to cook his food quickly. So he developed a way to prepare his secret recipe by dropping the chicken into a pressure cooker instead of frying it in a pan the way all his competitors were doing. This made the chicken extra crispy—the way we still know and love it today. But then came the perfect storm: a highway was built that bypassed Sanders's gas station/restaurant altogether. His dream was derailed, and he was forced to sell his business and live off his savings, teaching his recipe to a friend and allowing him to serve it in his restaurant. The friend's restaurant flourished, and Sanders knew that he was really onto something. So he packed his bags and went from restaurant to restaurant with a pressure cooker and some seasoning, in hopes of franchising his recipe. He slept in his car, took free meals from the restaurants he visited whenever possible, and slowly but surely his persistence began to pay off. Eventually word spread: people loved his recipe, and potential franchisees started coming to him. He shipped his spices to franchised restaurants at four cents on every chicken sold and eventually sold his share of the company for $2 million (which would be $15 million today). Eventually he moved to Canada to oversee the Canadian branches of his company, and until his death, he continued building his business into the monolith that is KFC.

Was Colonel Sanders born powerful? No. Was he given a handout? Of course not. He chased success down like a dog and didn't stop running until he caught it. As you are reading this right now, you may have an idea that people are telling you is crazy. I'm sure many people told Colonel Sanders he was crazy. But in the end, your results will vindicate you, no matter how crazy your idea seems or how many people you might have to alienate in pursuing it.

Can you cold-call businesspeople you find interesting? Are you willing to sleep in your car, pound the pavement, and never rest? I hope that the answer is yes. Because if you don't have that same dedication to your vision, I will never hear of you and you will never have the success and the power that you deserve. This is where the gulf exists between those who become powerful and the rest. Even if you lack everything else—resources, connections, even talent—but you can retain this endurance and persistence, and *never* give up, you can seize power. I can all but guarantee that you don't have it any harder than Sanders or any of the other figures we'll speak about later in this book. They did it. And so can you.

Now let's get into the practical strategies for attaining power and keeping it. I call these the Power Tools.

BEGIN WHEN YOU ARE YOUNG

The way we teach our children to think about power is incredibly important. It has a huge influence later in life. What does playing with the Hulk, Thor, and other action figures teach a child about power? What about playing with Barbie? I don't think it takes a child psychologist to figure this out.

When we are taught to pursue power from a young age, we become more confident, powerful, and reassured adults. There are many aspects of the modern self-esteem movement that I think are misguided. Telling kids that everyone gets a trophy for participating does nothing to prepare them for the real world, and this will only lead to disappointment later. Kids must be taught about the world as it is, not as we would like it to be. They must also be taught that success is important and empowered to understand that they *can* succeed.

Do you give your children a weekly allowance for doing nothing? Stop it. You're training them to expect that money will just magically appear when they need it. It doesn't work this way in the real world. Instead, teach them that nothing will happen for them unless they work for it. This will be especially important once they leave home at eighteen or so.

When I think back on the moments from my childhood that turned me into the powerful adult I am today, I always end up thinking about the hardest moments. In today's world, children are being given a free pass from hardship. We worry that too much homework is bad for them, that their schoolwork is too hard, that their classes start too early. We are preparing them for a world that doesn't exist. When parents try to give their kids the things they never had, they end up doing more harm than good. Providing a cushy life for your kids is going to be more of a curse than a blessing in the long run.

Instead, teach your kids, from an early age, to prepare for adulthood. Because if you're not planning your own future, you will become part of someone else's plan for their future. I think it's a shame that classes on accounting, taxes, and job hunting are not mandatory in high school. But this is the world as it is. You have an obligation to make sure that your children learn about these things. Teach them that the world isn't going to give them the life they want—they must help themselves. And if you want to give your children a weekly allowance, give them a quarter. After all, they already have all the food they can eat, you buy them most anything they want, and they have a roof over their head. For free.

Warren Buffett's father was incredibly strict with money, giving young Warren only five cents a week as allowance (which, even adjusted for inflation, is not very much). His father didn't have much money himself, but he taught Warren the power that money carries and instilled in him a value system that launched the man he would become. Buffett passed this on to his own children—Buffett plans to donate most of his fortune to the Bill and Melinda Gates Foundation upon his death; his children have some modest stock in Berkshire Hathaway, but for the most part they must fend for themselves.

If my kid asks me for a dollar on Monday morning and I fork it over without a care in the world—because, *c'mon,* it's a dollar—what happens on Tuesday morning after he has gone out and spent that dollar on a Ring Pop? Other than the fact that his teeth will be rotting, he will have developed the belief that money is a flowing faucet in my house. And then, when he grows up, he will have no value system in place to regulate his cash flow.

BE CONFIDENT

Even before you earn a single dollar, before you land that dream job, power exists. Power existed before you came into the world, and it will exist after you exit the world. It also exists whether you access it or not. Power, for the purposes of this book, is *the ability to make things happen.* It is the ability to walk into an unfamiliar room and "own it." Before you walk into the boardroom, or the bedroom, or any room, what is the single most important thing you can walk in with?

Confidence in yourself.

Without confidence, goals and tasks seem impossible, and become impossible. You must exude confidence for others to have confidence in you. There is an old saying: the door-to-door vacuum cleaner salesman is not selling vacuums. He is selling himself. You must embody the type of power you wish to possess *before* you possess it. Power is more than having a lot of money, though money helps immensely. Your personality and the world's perception of you translate to a sort of raw power that is hard to quantify.

DRESS FOR POWER

You know what I mean, don't you? Do I have to spell it out? We don't think about these things much. It's not *Mad Men,* and we don't all wear suits anymore. Today it's politically incorrect to tell people that their appearance and how they dress matters. But it's true.

Gentlemen, don't wear your jeans midway down your butt. From what I hear, this fashion statement started in prisons, where the "catcher" would advertise availability to those who were "pitchers." While I'm not judging anyone's sexual preferences, I am saying that a fashion statement that started as a way to advertise sexual submission in prison might not be the best thing to lead with in a professional setting. I'm sure you understand. It's hardly the message you want to send. Or maybe you do. It's your choice. This look will not make people think you're powerful. You may think you look cool, but the rest of the world will think (pardon my bluntness) that you're an idiot, uneducated, and possibly a criminal. I'm not saying that you *are* any of these things, but I'm talking about the way people will see you in the real world. Whether they're right or wrong is irrelevant. You will still have to deal with the consequences. Most important, you won't get a decent job dressed this way.

If you want to get ahead at work, dress like your boss. Dress for the job you want. If you work on Wall Street, your boss likely wears a suit and tie, so you need to be wearing a suit and tie, whether you feel like it or not. Whether a suit and tie expresses your "inner truth" or not. You may feel like coming in to work dressed like a Jimmy Buffett Parrothead, but I'd advise against it. Millennial CEOs like Mark Zuckerberg seem to prefer dressing for work in T-shirts, jeans, and hoodies. This is an expression of the rules and the culture in their organizations. And that's fine. If you work at Facebook, you don't need to come to work in a three-piece suit. But the rule still applies: *Dress like your boss.* Whether he/she wears a suit or jeans. People want to know that you are there to take your job seriously. Your clothes should communicate that. Before anyone speaks to you, before they know what you're selling, before they know anything about you at all, they are going to *see you*. And you have the opportunity to seize the upper hand in the power dynamic.

"Judge not, that ye be not judged." That's a nice quote from the New Testament. But it is *irrelevant*. We *do judge*. We *all do*. And we will all probably continue to do it. This is the way people are. So you can complain about it, or you can accept it and find a way to make it work for you. Before you ascend to any level of power, before you earn a dollar, people will *see you*. *People will judge you*. Based on your appearance, your attitude, your posture, your hygiene. They *will judge you* and try to determine how useful you are, what you can offer them.

Imagine yourself lost in an unfamiliar city. You want to find a phone, ask directions, perhaps get a room for the night. On one side of the street is a brightly lit, well-manicured hotel with well-dressed staff visible through its large windows. On the other side of the road is a decrepit-looking motel with peeling paint and shady characters standing around outside. Where are you going to seek shelter for the night? The answer is pretty obvious, and you came to this conclusion based on appearances.

The staff at the decrepit motel may be doing their best to maintain their business, but the only thing that matters is whether it appeals to you, the customer. On the flip side, you may approach the brilliantly lit hotel to find that the staff is standing at the entrance with their arms crossed, staring at you in an intimidating manner. I'm sure you're going to think twice about entering that building. Now, try to think of a person who is powerful and intimidating. I'm sure you know one. I sure do. Usually, it's me. On the surface, this seems like a bad strategy. However, you must dress and act the part for the business and the brand you have created. For me, being aggressive and off-putting works, because it is consistent with my brand. Similarly, the income model at that fancy hotel may depend on a feeling of exclusivity. This is not personal, nor is it an attack on a class of people. It is simply the business model that works best for the hotel. If that model stops working, the company that owns the hotel will immediately change its strategy.

The same goes for your appearance. Whatever you choose as your public persona, your hairstyle and your style of dress must be tailored to what will make you the most money and garner you the most power. If the way I dress began to have a negative effect on my ability to make deals, I would change my look *immediately*. You need to be willing to do the same thing. There are ways to dress the part, even if you lack the budget. You can court an aesthetic without going for the name on the label. We live in America, and there are plenty of discount options. Once you have money, investing in your appearance is a worthwhile expense. I'm not talking about trying to look handsome or sexy, though these things can help. I mean dressing for the level of power you wish to achieve. Dress like the people whose jobs you are after.

GET BETTER FRIENDS

"Show me your friends and I'll show you your future." This quote has been attributed to various people. What it means is that as you progress toward the person you want to become and accumulate power in all facets of your life, some of your old friends and acquaintances may not fit into your plan. Once again, what I am saying might offend your delicate sensibilities. And that's too bad. In our socially liberal society, we may care about each other's feelings, but *real life* doesn't care. The real world is a Darwinian place: only the strongest survive. Roll with the punches or be knocked down.

I'm not saying this because I take some kind of pleasure in judging your friends. I'm saying this because I want you to know that powerful people must make sacrifices. And you must be aware of friends who will bring you down during your pursuit of power. The further you advance, the more these people will reveal themselves. I've seen too many would-be successful people fizzle out because a couple of their buddies started calling asking for money, wanting a drinking partner, wanting to send them down the rabbit hole. Lose the bum friends who hang around you only to bring you down. Lose the drinkers who are only focused on having a bar buddy. Most of all, lose the swindlers who will latch on to you the moment you get some money before they've sucked you dry.

"But he's my best friend," you say. Unless he is helping you to gain power, *no, he is not*. In addition, you *will* be judged by the company you keep. Hang out with people who are more successful than you and people who are better looking than you. They go to better parties. They know other powerful people and they will take you places you may not get to by yourself. Yes, that means spending less time with the people you like but who can do nothing for you. Machiavellian? Manipulative? Insincere? Why, yes, all of the above. And it works.

You must decide here and now if your goal is to maintain the friendships you already have or if your goal is to seize power. Once you have achieved your goals, your less connected, less powerful friends may still be there—or they may not be. But you have a single life, a single body, and a single legacy to consider, and you must do with it what you must to make your dreams come true. Sometimes that means saying good-bye to people who cannot help you. Your friends should be a snapshot of who you want to become in the coming months and years. The herd in which you travel converges on shared values, and if you run with the herd that values power and success, you are more likely to become powerful and successful. If you run with a herd that values relaxation, pleasantries, going to the bar and having a beer, lying around and watching sports, guess what? That's all you are likely to achieve in that herd.

SPEAK ENGLISH AND SPEAK IT WELL

Communication is key to power. The better you sound speaking English, and the more convincing you are when you speak, the more you will enhance the perception of your power.

The most powerful figures throughout history, from civil rights leaders like Martin Luther King Jr. to saints, sinners, despots, and even Gandhi, had the gift of gab. Your initial impression of a person, right after the way he looks, comes from the way he speaks.

Language is important, and at the moment, the English language is most important, on a global scale. If this offends you, read this part carefully. I am not making a *value judgment* on English as *superior* to other languages. America is the greatest country in the world—I'll spar with anyone on that point. But that's not what I'm trying to say here. Not only is it incorrect to say that I'm promoting English as "better," but *these hurt feelings are a waste of time*. This is about *pragmatism*. Tomorrow, if Mandarin becomes the dominant language on the planet, guess who is going to be opening his Mandarin 101 book that evening? Me. I speak multiple languages because they are *useful*, not because I like one better than the other.

GO WHERE THE POWER IS

Have you ever noticed that successful people all seem to know one another? Work out at the same gym? Eat at the same restaurants? Belong to the same clubs? If you answered yes, then my question to you would be . . . why aren't you there? "It's too expensive," you may say. Okay, then apply for a job or an internship in one of these places. Find a way in, in any way that you can. Don't wait for an invitation. Cold-call people like Elon Musk did, go hang out in the clubs where your heroes play like Dave Grohl did, or pester people for internships like Warren Buffett did (I'll tell you their stories later in the book). Ask for advice. Ask to shadow your hero for a day. Ask and you may receive. But you won't get anywhere if you don't ask.

I was proud to be invited to ring the bell at the New York Stock Exchange. I'm not telling you about this to show off. I'm telling you because I want you to understand the reason I was invited to ring the bell: because I choose to put myself in the company of decision-makers and CEOs, and this leads to opportunity. When you keep this kind of company, you will do better in life, and you will expose yourself to many more opportunities than if you were, for example, sitting next to all the wonderful people in a baseball stadium watching a game. The hot dog you are eating may be delicious and the game you're watching may be entertaining, but nothing you are doing will help you to advance up the ladder of power.

That's right: your recreational activities are one of the things holding you back. "But that's my life, it's what I do for fun," you say. Business *is life*. It is *everything*. You should be that excited about your next *project, your dreams*. Everything else is a waste of time. Follow your dreams, not your empty pleasures. Otherwise you will spend, spend, spend, have some fun, and then die without having achieved anything.

PRACTICE

Everything on Earth obeys the same gravitational pull. If you bench-press a hundred pounds, it'll be the same hundred pounds for the next guy. But there's a difference in effort for the guy who's pumping three hundred pounds daily. When he goes to lift the hundred, it's going to feel quite light for him. That only comes with repetition and obsession. The same goes for every industry and skill set. When Steven Spielberg decides to make a film, do you think he begins to sweat and worry whether people are going to like it or if it will do well in the theaters? Of course not—he's lifted that weight fifty times before. When Tom Brady throws the ball forty yards up the field toward his receiver, do you think he worries about whether the throw will be completed? No, because he's repeated this motion infinite times, until it became part of him. Practice is the commonality among successful people. Practice over and over again, until you achieve exemplary results.

Say you want to become a rock star. Other than being able to brush off the endless criticism you'll incur along the way, you must be willing to practice, and perfect, endlessly. Think back to Dave Grohl. He couldn't afford music lessons, but he sat in his room and listened to Beatles records, and he imitated what he heard with a rabid, unceasing dedication to the instruments he loved, until he *figured it out*. With whatever skill you intend to use to pursue power, you must be obsessed with it enough to never tire of *trying to practice and perfect*. As a kid, maybe you were sold the nonsense that talent is what counts. This is untrue. Talent is nothing without hard work. Be talented at working hard and you can eventually be talented at almost anything else that interests you.

What does practice take away from the rest of your life? Well, the answer is time. So what are you willing to sacrifice to make time to practice? Most likely, you will not be able to wake up at noon and float your way to becoming a prodigy. You have to be willing to make the time and to wake up with the roosters. Even at my level, when KISS is touring, we return to the hotel after a show and we sleep, because we have to be up and on the move to our next location the following day. Five A.M. call times are not unheard-of on tour. Get over it, and get on with it. No excuses.

ALWAYS KEEP MOVING

This section is going to be most relevant for those of you who have already achieved success on some level. Success is wonderful, but like everything else in life, it can be fleeting. So a slight play on the old, familiar advice applies: after you first *succeed*, try, try again. I firmly believe that you should *never retire* if you can help it. Retirement as a concept came into being in 1881, and the retirement age was about the same as life expectancy, which basically means that reaching retirement was not the norm.

Not only are we living longer now than ever before, but the story surrounding retirement has changed significantly. We're now sold retirement as a goal to work toward. Something to look forward to. Let me tell you: if your life goal is to sit around and watch television, this book is not for you. Dave Grohl could have retired after Nirvana. Elon Musk could have retired after selling his first or second company, or revolutionizing one or two industries. If you're looking forward to retirement, you don't have a powerful enough goal in life. Find a better goal—a dynamic goal, one that makes you excited to get out of bed every morning—and you're not going to give retirement a second thought. Retirement, to me, is more terrifying than death.

PERSPECTIVE

Action is what matters. But the way you view the world will directly inform how you behave in it, how you react to hardship and success, and your ability to harness power. So let's take those blinders off and learn some hard truths.

LIFE IS NOT FAIR AND THE WORLD DOES NOT CARE ABOUT YOU

I'm not the first person to say this, and I won't be the last. But it bears repeating. Life is not kind or fair. I didn't make these rules. I'm just aware of them, and that is what gives me power. "All men are created equal" is one of those American ideals we are told to believe in, and it is a nice sentiment. But it is patently untrue. In almost every case—every facet of life, biology, society, physics, etc.—it is untrue. In fact, a more accurate statement might be "all men are created equally unequal." Some of us are born taller. Some are born shorter. Some of us are able to run faster. And some are naturally slow. And some of us are born smarter. That's right. Some people's DNA naturally makes them smarter. However, it's worth noting that members of Mensa (the organization that recognizes and lists those very bright people) are not necessarily the most powerful or rich. Being "book smart" does not necessarily equal wealth or power. By contrast, people who are the least intelligent by traditional standards can end up being the most powerful and rich. And that's because they have other characteristics that enable them to excel. The will to win. The will to learn. The will to never give up. The will to work harder and longer hours than the guy next to you.

We may not all be born with intellectual gifts, but we can all work longer and harder and smarter. The worst student in class can end up more powerful and rich than the straight-A student, if he plays his cards right. There are certain shortcomings that can be overcome with effort, hard work, and perhaps some luck. These are the stories we often cite when we make claims like, "You can do anything you set your mind to." Some shortcomings, however, cannot be overcome with effort. Some things *are actually impossible.* Fortunately or unfortunately, the only way to gain the wisdom to know the difference between the impossible and the possible is to try, to work very hard, and to fail—*a lot.*

But the fact remains that we do not start on equal footing from birth. Whether we think life *should be fair* is irrelevant. In fact, I believe that life *should not be fair,* even if we had the power to wave a magic wand and make it all fair. As a species, unfair circumstances are, counterintuitively, our greatest strength. Darwin showed us that evolution throws things at the wall to see what sticks. Whatever survives the harsh slings and arrows of reality gets passed on to the next generation. And this process makes us stronger. Harsh, unfair circumstances are the very reason we are here, with legs and brains and immune systems and problem-solving skills.

Unfairness, hardship, asymmetry: these are sources of pressure, and pressure turns coal into diamonds. This is a concept that, sadly, we seem to be on the verge of forgetting in this country. The more compassionate we become, the more we cater to one another's feelings, and the more we attempt to make life easier for the less fortunate—though these are all worthy endeavors— the more we forget that these utopian ideals are *not the natural order of things*. The further we manage to get from the feral reality of natural selection and competition, the less prepared we are to face the realities of our world. Nature may be cruel, but this is neither *right nor wrong*. Nature simply is, and we must be aware of and prepared for this fact in our quest to gain power.

Political correctness tells us that nothing is more important than the *way people feel*. If something offends us, if it hurts our feelings, if it makes us feel that we have been treated unfairly, it is to be *shunned and snuffed from the public discourse*. We believe this because we are trying to love one another. Because the road to hell is paved with good intentions, and we are afraid: afraid of failure, afraid of feeling sad or angry or bitter, afraid of not accomplishing our goals or seizing our dreams, afraid of death. We want to construct an artificial world around us made of packing peanuts that will shield us from these negative and necessary parts of life, but in doing so, we leave ourselves unprepared for the realities of the world. When they hit, they are that much more surprising, that much more brutal, and that much more devastating.

This is not a new concept. At some point in the late sixties, the *self-esteem movement* emerged. People decided (some say due to the guidance of a psychologist named Nathaniel Branden) that *feeling good about yourself* was positively correlated with real-world success and real-world results. This view is inherently solipsistic—the world *does not care if it makes you sad* or affects your self-esteem. The world is an unfeeling series of facts that you must come to terms with or ignore at your own peril. Self-esteem is certainly a positive emotion, and I already espoused that *confidence in yourself* is your first and most useful tool when you begin your journey. But *self-awareness* and awareness of the real world and its rougher edges are the next steps, and more useful.

We hand out participation trophies and tell kids that they've succeeded as long as they tried their best. But imagine if a surgeon said, "Well, I wasn't talented enough to perform that heart surgery. I've never been very good at it, and the patient died. But I really tried my best, and that's all that matters." This would be unacceptable. A person with this attitude would never even make it through medical school to become a surgeon. That person would fail, and failure in this case *would be a good thing*. Because people who think that doing their best is good enough *should not be allowed to perform heart surgery*. Unfair? Incredibly. And, incidentally, *good for the world*.

Trying your best is not as important as results. *Consequences* are important. Hard work and trying one's best are merely strategies to *get results*. Teaching someone correct sprinting form is the first step toward winning a race, but actually crossing the finish line first is what determines whether that person actually *wins the race*. No one would know the names Usain Bolt or Michael Phelps, despite their flawless form and incredible fitness level, if they did not *win*.

Numerous articles and books have been written about the failure of the self-esteem movement. As with almost everything in this book, I'm not the first to plant a flag here. But in our quest for power, this source of weakness must be discarded. We must not conflate how useful self-esteem can be in *pursuing a goal* with the *goal itself*. A pile of wood, a hammer, and some nails is not the same as a house; they are just the first steps toward building a house, and they mean nothing if you do not finish the house or do not *build it well*.

In Shakespeare's plays, the fool or the court jester was often the only character who could speak the truth to the king, because he was a jokester who was not to be taken seriously. In the modern era, we can similarly look to our comedians for glimpses of the truth. Let us turn to a routine by the late, great, fire-tongued George Carlin on this topic:

All of this stupid bullshit that children have been so crippled by has grown out of something called the self-esteem movement . . . and I'm happy to say it has been a complete failure, because studies have repeatedly shown that having high self-esteem does not improve grades, does not improve career achievement, it does not even lower the use of alcohol, and it most certainly does not reduce the incidence of violence of any sort, because as it turns out, extremely aggressive, violent people think very highly of themselves. Imagine that, sociopaths have high self-esteem . . . I love when these politically correct ideas crash and burn . . . The self-esteem movement revolved around a single notion, the idea . . . that every child is special . . . Every child is clearly not special . . . But let's say it's true. Let's grant this . . . Isn't every adult special too? . . . And if every adult is special, then that means we're all special and the whole idea loses all its fucking meaning.

If it was true while Carlin was alive, it has almost certainly gotten worse now, in an age where political correctness and sensitivity are enforced to such a degree that many feel that their free speech is being infringed upon. We believe we are all special, that we are all entitled to "win" and "succeed." But if *everyone* wins, and if *everyone* is special, then almost by definition *no one wins, and no one is special.* If there are no boundaries between winning and losing, then winning and losing *are the same*. Every time you walk out your door and expect the world to cater to your fragile feelings and subtle, sensitive ideas about right and wrong, you rob yourself of power. It's a jungle out there. Being idealistic is fine, but being prepared is more useful and will allow you to navigate the world and use reality to your advantage, instead of being "oppressed" by it.

As I've said, the world is not fair, nor should it be. Some of us are just born smarter, but most of us are not Stephen Hawking, Michio Kaku, or Isaac Newton. I know that I'm not, nor will I ever be, though I may raise my station by careful study and hard work. On the flip side, some of us may not have book smarts, but are street smart. Put someone with street smarts in the middle of an unfamiliar city without a dollar in their pocket, and they will be able to clamber out of obscurity with just their wits and will. Others would be hopeless in this situation. That's just the way it is.

Some of us have neither book smarts nor street smarts and are simply *not very bright*. Period. It's harsh, but it's true. Some people out there are stupid—accept it. But regardless of where you are on Mother Nature's intelligence scale, you need to do what all animals in the wild do: adapt. Take your weaknesses as realities and acknowledge them, find your strengths, and *find a way*. Recognize that your situation is unfair and then get over it. Succeed *anyway*.

How, you ask? By being a chameleon. *Pretend* you're smarter, stronger, etc., by simply hanging out with the right crowd, changing your colors, faking it if you must, and reading and practicing *as much as you can,* as we've covered above. Unless you are watching the news, turn the TV off and pick up a book. Find out what smart people you admire are reading and read those books. Your brain is like a muscle that must be used in order to grow. Incidentally, the fool who takes it upon himself to read relentlessly, to educate himself, and to work hard is much more valuable to the job market than the genius who lies around all day, navel-gazing and exerting minimal effort.

Hard work is more important than talent or intelligence. Hard work is your trump card. However, you will not accomplish anything until you have first come to terms with the *reality* of your shortcomings—intellectual, physical, or whatever they may be. If you know you're bad at something, if you *know* where your brain falls short, you are ahead of the game and that much closer to fixing and/or getting around your flaw. The self-esteem movement, participation trophy culture, and political correctness all get in the way of honest self-criticism and true self-improvement.

FEMALE SEXUALITY IS POWER

Everything in the world is about sex except sex. Sex is about power.

—Oscar Wilde

Being powerful is like being a lady. If you have to tell people you are, you aren't.

—Margaret Thatcher

As long as we are being politically incorrect, there is another elephant in the room that must be addressed. There is an intangible kind of power that we haven't discussed yet and that can translate into success, into dollar signs, and into the ability to get things done. This kind of power has nothing to do with your title or your career, nor does it have anything to do with honest hard work. It is another way in which the world as it exists is *not fair*. Across cultures, across time, across civilizations and continents and oceans:

Power resides wherever there are beautiful women. *Women specifically.*

The sexuality of beautiful women has long been coveted in a way that men's sexuality simply is not. This is an obsession that transcends nationality and culture, and manifests itself throughout every corridor of power, in healthy and unhealthy ways. Now, in our politically correct culture, it is generally taboo for me, an older male, to even broach this topic. But anyone who knows me knows I don't care about taboos. If this discussion offends you, it stands to reason that you do not have what it takes to interact with the real world outside of a very narrow, liberal bubble. And that's okay, as long as you live in an area that supports that bubble (which, incidentally, requires people in power to maintain it—funny how that works). However, the real world tends to intrude, whether we want them to or not, and we need to face some very real facts about the differences between men and women, whether we like them or agree with them. So let's continue, and I beg of you, keep an open mind. Not everything that smacks of conservative traditionalism is simply wrong.

Many of our violations of political correctness actually contain a *grain of truth*.

Generally speaking, men pursue women. The more a man succeeds in his (*consensual*) pursuit of women, the more social power he gains. A man's *ability* to grab the attention of beautiful women can be used to gain more power. In addition, if you are considered a beautiful woman, *that* is a source of power, because you are in demand, like it or not. A beautiful woman can walk through the doors of the most exclusive club, while her male counterpart will be stopped at the velvet rope. There are lots of things we are tempted to say when confronted with this inconvenient truth, such as "Everyone is beautiful" or "Beauty is subjective." This is a way of being compassionate to everyone's feelings, but it's a sentiment that is ultimately useless to you. Because it doesn't reflect reality, and in reality, not everyone is beautiful *to everyone*. Whether it's the result of biology, genetics, or cultural conditioning, there is a certain *look,* particularly in women, that commands attention on a massive scale. It sells cars, movies, clothing, magazines, and food. It *works*.

You can try to make yourself feel better, try to improve your self-esteem, by telling yourself that it's all *bullshit* and that everyone is beautiful and that it's what's *inside* that counts. That's fine to do. It might be the mentally healthier option. Or you can acknowledge the unfair reality that *female beauty is a form of power,* and then do your best to *use* it to your advantage. If you are a woman, you can choose to make yourself as beautiful as you can. If you are a man, you can surround yourself with beautiful women, if you can. If you do this successfully (and not everyone is able to), it can benefit you enormously.

Hugh Hefner built an entire empire on this concept. Throughout his entire life, he has remained *on brand:* he surrounds himself with beautiful women, which has a twofold effect. Many straight men, of course, want to *be* him, and have wanted to be him for generations. Women, in some cases, disapprove. But in other cases, women see a man in very high demand with women who are even better looking than they are, and in this demand there is a form of power. Women over the years have *wanted* him because he *was wanted* by other women. This effect can be seen in Hollywood heartthrobs, rock stars, and the like. Many of us rock stars, in particular, aren't actually very good-looking in the traditional sense. I'm a prime example of how this kind of power works. I was some people's cup of tea when I was young, but I was always a strange-looking guy, even out of costume. Some of us rock musicians are downright goofy looking. However, we find a way to be *in demand* with women. We get onstage, we strap a guitar to our chests, and we embrace our individuality and *own it,* with *confidence.* We say, "Yeah, that's right, I'm weird looking, and I'm *hot, and women love me.*" This really does work, if you can be convincing in the way you put this out there. Once you have established yourself as someone who is "good with women," there is a kind of domino effect: *other women* begin to want you, despite your physical shortcomings. This is why the cliché of the rich, powerful old man with an

Anna Nicole on his arm exists. Some call it charisma, some credit money. Whatever it is, it is *powerful*.

I made a living *spitting blood*, sticking my tongue out, and being as *grotesque and horrifying as possible* as part of my onstage persona. It appealed to men, sure, as a sort of horror-movie spectacle, as a pagan deity of sorts. But it also appealed to women. KISS was famous, in our single days, for our dalliances with groupies, and I rarely attempted to pretty myself up in the traditional sense, because I did not need to. I was *in demand with women,* because I was onstage and because I commanded *power.* The dominos fell—women wanted me because other women wanted me. Because I *owned the room.* If you can create this perception, of being wanted by women, then other women will begin to want you, whether the initial impression is true or not. If women want you or if women want what you have, *people will pay attention to what you have to say.* Yes, offensive, but also, inconveniently, true.

If you are a woman, I must say something even harsher that will make me sound like a misogynistic blowhard. But please get past that knee-jerk reaction, because it is not your friend in the real world. *The world does not care how you think it should be.* If you want to affect social change and destroy the power dynamics that exist, more power to you—I'll support you. But I am not writing this book for a hypothetical utopia, where women are never judged by their appearance. I am writing this book in the real world, where women are objectified and seen as sexual objects—and this is a horrible thing when it is unwanted. But I'm trying to help you cope with a world that is not entirely fair, or just, or correct. I am trying to help you be an opportunist, to manipulate an unfair, unjust, incorrect world more effectively, more ruthlessly. So let me say this clearly: *Ladies, if you are interested in harnessing this type of power, first be honest with yourself about how you look.* That is to say, be honest with yourself about how you are perceived. And if you find that you have this power that is unique to your sex, *you should not feel ashamed to use it.*

People may look down on you or try to shame you for it. Do not listen to them. Your goal is power, and using all of your resources, including manipulating society's expectations of your sexuality and your gender, is part of gaining power. I am not making a value judgment on whether society or men or people in general are *morally correct* in the way they view you or limit you based on these preconceived notions of who you are. I am merely pointing out the reality and reminding you that this reality, fair or unfair, can be used to your advantage if you so choose.

The more socially enlightened among us will take great offense at my pointing out these traditional power dynamics. They will say, "Surely we are all equal. Surely this male-female, hunter-hunted thing is a remnant of the past." Absolutely not. It exists in the here and now, when the cameras are off and our self-censorship is at rest, because that is the space in which *life happens,* for better or for worse.

If you are a woman reading this, you may have a dilemma about your integrity. You want to be taken seriously for the gifts of your mind, and you want to achieve things and seize power without reference to your sexuality. There is a sense of disgust inherent in the idea of exploiting your sexuality for power, and there is a lot of pressure on women (often from other women) to reserve your sexuality, to hide it, to snuff it out, lest it give you an unfair advantage. How many times have you heard someone say something like, "She only got that job because she's well endowed," or "She's only successful because they want to sleep with her." Well, guess what? Whatever the reason, she's making it *work for her.*

On both ends, for the critic and for the woman being criticized, I know this must be frustrating. This is a situation with which I sympathize, but of course, I cannot truly empathize, because I'm not in your shoes. This is the cross you may have to bear in the world as it currently exists. There are people making strides in these areas, but change is always slow, and in the meantime, we still have to go to work and live our lives.

As the world currently stands, you must choose. Is it worth it to you to use your sexuality to your advantage? Or will you choose to purposefully stifle your sexuality and its inherent power, and try to make sure that your success is entirely dependent on your work ethic, your mind, and your talents? If you are traditionally beautiful, there will likely come a time when you will need to choose between one of these two roads. It is your prerogative to decide whether using us men and our beastly ways to achieve power is worth it to you. You'd be surprised what just a suggestion from your lips can make us do. And you can choose to ignore the puritanical voices in your head that say that it is "evil" and "immoral" to embrace your sexuality and use it where it most benefits you.

I happen to think these taboos are nonsense. If you have the ability to marshal an aspect of yourself to get what you want, I say you should go for it, and this includes sexuality and being sexually desired. Modesty be damned. I believe that our distaste for this sort of thing stems from jealousy. Men are jealous if they can't have you. Other women are jealous because they can't do what you can do or are too ashamed. When I encourage you to ignore all of this societal pressure, I am not making a moral argument. Consensual sex, in any context, is okay. People worry about it too much. Worrying about whether someone is going to call you a "slut" is a *waste of time*. Because guess what? I've gotten high-fives for the very same behavior that gets you called a slut. The people calling you names just don't want you to have the same amount of fun that I had. I say go for it. Join me. And ignore the critics. Do whatever it takes to win.

MEN AND WOMEN ARE DIFFERENT

This section is for the ladies. It covers how I believe power dynamics differ for men and women. If you are a woman, you may not be interested in my thoughts on the matter. And that's fine, skip this part. But do so at your own risk. I may not know the first thing about what it's like to be a woman, but I do know a thing or two about seizing power. So it might be to your benefit to lend an ear, even if you get offended in the process.

In addition to the sexual power that women possess, there is another source of pressure on women today. As a woman, society tells you that you are supposed to have a boyfriend and get married by a certain age, or else you are simply not valuable. And it is still seen as perfectly socially acceptable to lean on your spouse if you are a woman. Men, on the other hand, are under a lot more social pressure to be independently successful. And that pressure is a good thing. It's what drives us toward power. Women, you are not going to attain the power you want out of life by relying on your boyfriend or your husband. So I say this social pressure should be expanded to include both sexes. It makes us stronger, as individuals and as a society.

Ladies out there who are reading this book, you *deserve* to be powerful. Make that part of your mind-set. Shifting your mind-set is the first step toward actually acquiring power. When you kick that sorry-ass boyfriend or husband to the curb for breaking your heart, I don't want you to be left heartbroken, scared, or unprepared to take life by the scruff of the neck and make it bend to your will. You will need the tools and strategies in this book to become the rich and powerful woman you deserve to be. The fact remains that in our society, at the moment, men are viewed as more aggressive and competitive. Whether you attribute this to cultural brainwashing, systemized misogyny, testosterone, or DNA, I don't care. I'm only concerned that you acknowledge the reality of the situation. Do you wish that things were different? I'm sure that you do. But pretending that they are is not going to do anyone any good.

If you want to change things, I am not suggesting that you inject yourself with testosterone, especially now that we understand that you will probably start growing hair in places you may not want. But be aware that your *natural inclination* to be a nurturer and to avoid conflict may not be what you need to compete and succeed in the "World of Man." And I capitalized that phrase, because I don't want you to kid yourself. Civilization in the world we live in, so far, has always been and continues to be built by the hand of *man,* by a pretty huge majority. And yes, I know people like to argue that without women, mankind would not exist. Technically, they are right. But what good is winning an argument if you are not going to walk away with power? There's still a big bad world of traditional ideas out there. That's a fact. Complaining about how unfair and awful it is *will not make you powerful.*

So, ladies, enough with the "I gotta get married or I'll become an old maid" nonsense. You are going to have to decide early in your twenties whether you want a family or a career. Because pragmatically speaking, being pregnant will take you out of the workforce, it will take a toll on you, and it will therefore make you less competitive. You are, most likely, not going to be able to have your cake and eat it too. While you are pregnant with your beloved child, your male peers will be racing ahead of you, because it's simply easier with their circumstances. And after you give birth to your child, that child will take up a lot of your time and energy, but will not make you one ounce more powerful. My apologies for being so blunt. So, ladies, if you want to be powerful, I say this:

Career first. Family second.

Go and get your power. Go and get your money. Stop depending on men. They will invariably let you down. And when they leave you, because statistics tell us that most of them do, you will likely be unprepared to become the rich and powerful woman you always wanted to be, and should be. Quite frankly, the world would be a better place if the leaders of the countries of the world were women. Currently, that does not seem to be the case. Let's fix it. Regardless, if you are a woman, I want you to be powerful and rich.

Not with your man's money.

With *your* money.

Your power.

Wake up in the morning, make your own decisions, don't ask anyone if they would like coffee in bed. Have somebody bring *you* coffee in bed.

Step one is acknowledging the way the world is, even if it hurts your feelings. Step two is kicking the world in the ass and making it change.

6

THE CLASSICAL
POWER PANTHEON

**A wise man ought always to follow the paths
beaten by great men, and to imitate those who
have been supreme, so that if his ability does
not equal theirs, at least it will savour of it.**

—Niccolò Machiavelli

Power is everything. Everyone wants it, whether they admit it or not, and people respond strongly to those who have it, while they have it. This may sound villainous or immoral to you. But if you've decided to read this book, I ask that you open your mind to what you perceive to be the dark side for a moment. I promise, there will be something to learn there. Though I consider myself an authority on power, there have been many more powerful figures than myself throughout history who have expressed these principles far better than I ever could. In this section, we will explore a few classic, historic examples of power.

NICCOLÒ MACHIAVELLI

THE REALIST

We are much beholden to Machiavelli and others that write what men do, and not what they ought to do.
—Francis Bacon

In January 2013, Pulitzer Prize–winning author Jared Diamond told the *New York Times Book Review* that if he could recommend one book to the president of the United States, it would be Machiavelli's *The Prince*. As he told the *Times:*

> Machiavelli is frequently dismissed today as an amoral cynic who supposedly considered the end to justify the means. In fact, Machiavelli is a crystal-clear realist who understands the limits and uses of power. Fundamental to his thinking is the distinction he draws between . . . the sphere in which a statesman can influence his world by his own actions [and] the role of chance beyond a statesman's control. But Machiavelli makes clear . . . that we are not helpless at the hands of bad luck. Among a statesman's tasks is to anticipate what might go wrong, and to plan for it. Every president (and all of us nonpoliticians as well) should read Machiavelli and incorporate his thinking.

Niccolò Machiavelli was born in Florence, Italy, in 1469, the son of Florentine nobility. He lived during a tumultuous time when Italy was divided into four competing city-states, and various popes battled with France, Spain, Switzerland, and the Holy Roman Empire for control of Italy. When he began his writing he was a junior squire, and even at this young age he observed the way that his fellow youths would *battle for superiority* in their social circles. He would eventually write in his *History of Florence* that his peers at the time made it a priority "to speak with wit and acuteness, whilst he who could wound others the most cleverly was thought the wisest." This observation has modern resonance. Think about any presidential debate you've seen in the past decade, or any schoolyard roast battle, or any competition between two men trying to impress a woman at a bar. Think about who tends to win: those who "wound others the most cleverly."

After the powerful Medici family fell in Italy, Machiavelli became a diplomat, and things were good for a while—he was climbing the rungs of power, one by one. The safest place for him to be was alongside the highest families in the state. As we've covered: *show me your friends and I'll show you your future*. In the free state of Florence, he did his best to ingratiate himself, though not without conflict, and to assimilate into the upper crust. This is a smart thing to do, and you should do it too. Not necessarily with politicians—you should hang out with anyone who has what *you* want. With the momentum he had, he was poised to gain real power and prestige. Yet it was not to be.

When an uprising restored the Medici family to power on September 14, 1512, Machiavelli's strategy of allegiance backfired. He was imprisoned for conspiracy against the Medicis, and he was physically tortured. The next time you think your life's unfair because you got fired, maybe think about what that must have been like for him. Maybe your rent is late and the debt collectors are calling, but it could be worse. The kind of torture that Machiavelli faced is worse than any of the problems we are likely to face in our quest for power today.

There is a lesson here as well. Above all, Machiavelli seemed to consider himself a realist, and so must you. He knew that life was unfair, and though one can guard oneself against the slings and arrows of fate in many ways and build the best suit of armor possible, there are forces of nature at work (which he referred to as "fortune") that sometimes upset all our plans, no matter how well we take advice or how smart we are or how strong we become. He knew that it was not only important to be prepared, but to roll with the punches when preparation fails. Even if you do everything right, shit still happens, if you'll pardon my French.

Machiavelli was eventually released from prison and permitted by the pope to formally retire in Tuscany. It was in the aftermath of these bitter and trying times that he did the writing that would eventually become his legacy. Another lesson exists here: If times are tough, and you can't seem to catch a break, *create a job or an occupation for yourself.* Find some way to use the resources and the abilities that you do have. There is no such thing as "free time," there is only more time in which to pursue the things you want. Machiavelli reflected on the tough realities he had experienced and wrote what would become the foundation of his most famous work, *The Prince*. At that point, he had witnessed firsthand how unfair the world could be and how cutthroat even the most civilized societies were at their core, especially within the ruling class.

Machiavelli was eventually approached by Cardinal Giulio de' Medici to write the history of Florence. Five years later, upon finishing the commission, he was on his way to restoring his name to good standing with the Medici family, and climbing back into power, even after all he had been through. Machiavelli had revived himself—and his good name—through his writings. Then, in 1525, following the Battle of Pavia, the French were defeated, Rome was sacked, and once more the Medici family was banished from Florence. Machiavelli returned to Florence in hopes of regaining his old position as secretary to the second chancery, but he fell ill and never got the chance. Again: do everything right, and reality will still, often, intrude. Life is unfair. Even for Machiavelli. He died in 1527 and was buried in the Church of Santa Croce in Florence, alongside some of the most influential Italians throughout history, including Galileo and Michelangelo. During his lifetime, he could never have imagined the level of renown that his writings would earn him, and today he is regarded by many as the founder of modern political science.

Not bad for someone who is popularly considered the author of the "bad guy" manifesto. In *The Prince*, Machiavelli famously asserts that when it comes to maintaining political power, the ends always justify the means—no matter how violent or immoral those means might be. Today, the term *Machiavellian* makes people think of power-hungry villains and their many abuses. Machiavelli's worldview is referred to as *consequentialism*. If you are someone who worries about the end result of your actions, and not quite as much about how you arrive at those ends, you may be a consequentialist. If you review the story of Machiavelli's life, you will recognize this worldview, which Machiavelli had to maintain because he was constantly juggling allegiances and ingratiating himself to one regime, only to have that regime toppled by another, and then toppled again. Was his constant shifting of alliances cowardly? I don't think so. In my view, it was practical. You do what you've got to do to succeed, in whatever world you find yourself in.

Today, *Machiavellian* is used to describe fictional characters like Tony Soprano, Frank Underwood from *House of Cards,* Lord Varys from *Game of Thrones,* Walter White in *Breaking Bad,* and, of course, retroactively, Iago in Shakespeare's *Othello*. These flawed "antiheroes" have seized our collective imagination, and we root for them while acknowledging that they do not always make the morally right decision. We root for them because we believe in their goals, even if we feel distaste for their means. Because we understand that the world is more complex and less perfect than we want it to be. Putting aside moral judgment for a moment, what do all these "villains" and "antiheroes" in fiction have in common? In my view, it's their ability to *get things done*. In the business world, we would call these characters "doers" if we met them. They are *productive,* for better or for worse, and this is one of the things we find compelling about them.

Reading *The Prince* inspired me to write this book, and I have a slightly different view of the term *Machiavellian* than many people do. When I read *The Prince,* I was fascinated by the descriptions I read of human nature, of how people behave, of how people in authority conduct themselves in the real world, and of how best to navigate this complex web. The reason I believe Machiavelli is important, and misunderstood, is because he was arguably one of the first writers to create a book that deals with people *the way they are,* as opposed to the way *we wish them to be. The Prince* asserts many shocking things as simple precepts, such as the idea that leaders should always mask their true intentions and "act against mercy, against faith, against humanity, against frankness, against religion, in order to preserve the state." Does this mean that Machiavelli is to blame for the violence and brutality that has racked the globe since he wrote his book? No. He was simply describing the world as it exists.

People have been lying, manipulating, cheating, destroying, and betraying each other since the beginning of time. Machiavelli wrote a book with this in mind, about how you get by in a world where this is true. Before Machiavelli, political thought was based on moral philosophy—in other words, abstract ideas about right and wrong, which in theory sounds like a good place to start. But the world is not ideal, and the history of human civilization tells us that societies rise and fall under the weight of human error, and corruption and violence are the norm. Human beings are capable of making speeches about the highest virtue, only to commit the most heinous crimes the moment they leave the podium. "But it's wrong," you say, "it's not fair." You are absolutely right. So what now? Deny it? Pretend the world is fair? Or do you move forward with this *knowledge*? Machiavelli accepts that people lie, cheat, and manipulate, that it's part of human nature. Instead of *shunning* these activities, he *accepts* them as an inevitable part of human existence and tells the reader how to sidestep and counter them. He says, "There is such a gap between *how* one lives and how one *should* live that he who neglects what is being done for what *should* be done will learn his destruction rather than his preservation" (emphasis mine).

More than anything else, Machiavelli seems to have intended to write a practical guide on how one may come to rule. In the context of the book you're reading now, "ruling" need not apply to nations. It can be applied to social, political, and professional settings, as well as to relationships. It is important to note that Machiavelli wrote *The Prince* in simple, easy-to-understand language. He wrote in Italian, not in Latin, which was the traditional written language at the time, in a move made for the sake of accessibility. Dante Alighieri, of *Inferno* fame, did the same thing. Both authors used what was then the common language in order to have their message reach the greatest number of people, as opposed to just a select cultural elite. The lesson here is that power lies in the masses, not in the niche. Whatever you want to achieve in the world, you should cast the widest net and have your approach be understandable and accessible to as many people as possible. Apple and Microsoft deal in computers, which were initially thought to be too complex and advanced for the common person. But through their sleek, simple interfaces and designs, these companies made computers easy to use, and an entire world revolving around the "personal computer" was born. Do this with language, do this with your product, do this with yourself. The *masses* are the only source of real power.

Many argue that *The Prince* was intended to be satire, which is to say that it was intended to criticize dishonest rulers. Machiavelli devotes considerable effort to describing all the crucial mistakes a tyrant can make, with numerous passages about how to usurp such a ruler. For our purposes, it does not matter whether *The Prince* is intended as satire. It is a book about seizing power and how one can succeed and fail at it. Both sides in any conflict can read this work and glean strategy from it. And even if it is satire, the strategies, the subterfuge, and the tenacity described in *The Prince* all tend to *work*. Indeed, Machiavelli's strategies have worked till today, though because of the negative press his name garners, public figures rarely admit it. It would be hard for me to describe a modern figure as Machiavellian without getting dragged into a Twitter argument.

Regardless, let's examine the strategies themselves and see if they sound familiar.

PUBLIC PERSONA IS IMPORTANT

In *The Prince,* Machiavelli describes politicians who court an appearance of being virtuous and idealistic while acting cynical/realistic in their policies. I don't think I have to name names for this to sound familiar. Insert any politician or businessman's name here. There are countless who come to mind. The fact remains that your reputation is a source of *power,* and if your past is a little checkered . . . that's what PR companies are for. This idea, of course, leads Machiavelli to suggest that lying and deceiving are often necessary in order to garner public support. This conflict can be seen in our modern political process. Should we be shamelessly idealistic about the way we present ourselves, and possibly unsafe as a result? Or should we be pragmatic and compromise, or postpone, our higher virtues in favor of safety? Machiavelli suggests the latter with the appearance of the former, in order to sway public opinion. This is where he gets into trouble with critics.

Pop culture has tackled this question. Consider the ending of Christopher Nolan's *The Dark Knight*. Batman takes all the blame for Harvey "Two-Face" Dent's crimes so that his good name as a politician, and thus his shining example, will be preserved for the good of Gotham City and to maintain hope. In this sort of situation, I side with Machiavelli. A worthy end goal is sometimes worth deception, even mass deception. If you appear trustworthy, and if people *like you,* you will be able to get things done. Perhaps this is not very honorable. Perhaps it is deceptive to appear to be kind and magnanimous in your everyday affairs if your only goal *is to bolster your reputation*. But if we are consequentialists, the *end result* is the only thing that really matters. Machiavelli writes: "Everyone sees what you appear to be, few experience what you really are. And those few dare not gainsay the many who are backed by the majesty of the state."

I will become whatever kind of person I have to be to succeed. And so should you, because once you do succeed, if you really feel sore about how cynical the world is, you will have the power to change what you don't like about the ladder you climbed up on, *after* you reach the top. Remember: put your oxygen mask on first, then help your children. To change the world, you must first gain the power to change the world.

Let's try a more relatable example of deception. If your boss says, "Look how great I look in my new suit," it is my view that you'd better be ready to *suck up* whether he does or not. He holds the keys to the castle, and you want him to feel good around you. So yes, even if you hate his suit, you should *lie* to him, for the greater good of his self-esteem and your advancement. This is a lie everyone, more or less, can understand. Multiply that intuition a thousandfold and imagine the sorts of problems someone with true power, a world leader, a "prince," must face on a daily basis in order to preserve diplomacy. Imagine facing impossible choices, and imagine coming upon situation after situation in which doing something regrettable, and lying about it, is the best course of action to prevent something worse or to prepare for something better.

Welcome to the real world, where good guys must sometimes lie, where the underdog often loses to the powerful, and where we must all fight to survive.

But what if *you* are the boss in this scenario? This leads to our next lesson:

DO NOT SUCCUMB TO FLATTERY

Just as it is important for you to flatter your boss, to gain power over him and to advance your career, it is important, if you are the boss, not to fall for the same trick yourself. In this example, you can clearly see the value in looking at the world with eyes that are truly morally neutral—this is about strategy, strategy, strategy. Is the underling *wrong* for flattering the superior? Is the superior *wrong* for failing to see through flattery? Neither question is of much importance in *The Prince*. The only question that matters is whether flattery and/or seeing through flattery is *effective*.

Needless to say, flattery can blind us to someone's true intentions and to the truth itself. If someone is worried about offending you, they may withhold or distort information that may be vital to you, for fear of repercussions or hurting your feelings. If you work in a creative field, this is poison. In Hollywood, there is a saying that you can "die from encouragement." When a thousand people tell you the song you just recorded is "perfect" and "amazing," they're not responding to the song; they are responding to your presence and the feeling that pleasing you would be socially beneficial. You could go forward with that "perfect, amazing" song and sell exactly zero records, because the truth eluded you in a cloud of flattery. This kind of praise does you no favors. So encouraging people to tell you the *truth*, while walking the line to make sure they still respect your authority, is important if you are in a position of power. As Machiavelli puts it: "There is no other way of guarding oneself from flatterers except letting men understand that to tell you the truth does not offend you; but when every one may tell you the truth, respect for you abates."

And lest you think that Machiavelli's principles are only about the mean-spirited ways to seize power, I come to our next precept:

EDUCATE YOURSELF AND BE WELL-ROUNDED

This quote is my personal favorite, and I proudly spread this nugget of wisdom far and wide: "Take pains to study letters and music, for you see what honour is done to me for the little skill I have. Therefore, my son, if you wish to please me, and to bring success and honour to yourself, do right and study, because others will help you if you help yourself." Why, yes, this applies specifically to me, a sixth grade teacher turned musician who is not classically trained but nevertheless excelled in the field of rock and roll, which led me to rub shoulders with people in other fields who have achieved excellence, which in turn allowed me to explore those fields: investing, acting, running businesses, producing, and even writing books, for example. It applies to me, who learned to speak English as well and better than native-born Americans in order to succeed, because I knew what powerful people tend to *sound like*.

It worked: the pains I undertook were rewarded. The proof is in the pudding, as they say. Is it *manipulative* to study letters and music, and to study generally, for the purpose of "bringing success and honour" to myself, as opposed to doing it purely for the sake of knowledge? Is it devious to read for the sake of strategy rather than to read for pleasure? Maybe. But I want to succeed, and I will do whatever it takes and learn whatever I must learn. Education, no matter what field you wish to be a part of, no matter what kind of power you wish to gain, is your golden key: "To exercise the intellect the prince should read histories, and study there the actions of illustrious men, to see how they have borne themselves in war, to examine the causes of their victories and defeat, so as to avoid the latter and imitate the former."

Congratulations, you've already taken the first step by reading this book. You're on the path. Now keep going and keep reading—not just my book, but any book by any author who has something that you want. Turn off the TV—there is little power to be found there. Your house should look like a Barnes & Noble. No money to buy books? Libraries are free, as is the advice of librarians. Incidentally, libraries also have computers. In the age of information, there is no excuse to not self-educate.

ALWAYS PLAY IT SAFE: HOPE FOR THE BEST AND PREPARE FOR THE WORST

Not all people in power follow this precept. There are those who choose to gamble with their future and who owe, perhaps, as much of their success to luck as they do to their hard work and talent. Then again, Machiavelli tells us that we are all slaves to *fortune,* and just as we must be realistic about people and human nature, so too must we be realistic about the indifference of the universe. The world does not care about you. The universe does not care that you are here, and all of existence couldn't care less whether you succeed or accomplish your dreams.

It's time to leave that *law of attraction* bullshit on the curb for the garbageman. "Speaking things into existence" only works if you motivate yourself to then go out and *do something.* The world will always throw you curveballs, and you must not let yourself become complacent, even if you find yourself in a good place. When I want to demonstrate this principle, I'll ask the following question: How many wheels does a car come with? If you said four, you are incorrect. A car comes with *five wheels,* including the spare, usually found in the trunk. I then ask why, to which people usually respond: "For if you get a flat tire." This is also wrong. The spare is not for *if* you get a flat tire, it is for *when* you get a flat tire. What can happen will happen, and you are better off in finance, in business, and in life the more deeply you internalize this lesson. It is never a matter of *if* but always *when.* If you prepare, you will not be taken off guard when the unthinkable, the improbable, inevitably hits you right in the gut: "A wise prince ought to observe some such rules, and never in peaceful times stand idle, but increase his resources with industry in such a way that they may be available to him in adversity, so that if fortune chances it may find him prepared to resist her blows," Machiavelli tells us.

The fact that we still talk about *The Prince,* and the fact that in modern society we commonly use the term *Machiavellian,* is proof that, whether you approve or disapprove of the morality of Machiavelli's strategy, it *works.* This is the pragmatism I am asking you to consider with this book: look only to what actions *accomplish for you.* Your attention is best spent on action, on strategies that reliably allow you to accomplish your goals, despite the judgment of your inner critic or any outer ones. Machiavelli's precepts stand on their own, and when applied properly, you will be shocked at how power may suddenly become attainable.

NAPOLEON BONAPARTE

THE CONQUEROR

Death is nothing, but to live defeated and inglorious is to die daily.
—Napoleon Bonaparte

I chose Napoleon Bonaparte for this section precisely because of how obvious, how household, his name has become. Napoleon, in name, has become bigger than the man himself, and his legacy is rife with urban legend and misinterpretation. He is simultaneously regarded as one of history's greatest heroes and vilest villains. He has been called both the father of modern democracy and of fascism.

Napoleon was born on August 15, 1769, on a small island in the Mediterranean called Corsica. Around the time of Napoleon's birth, Corsica was attempting to gain independence and the French had invaded. Born under the umbrella of one war, Napoleon would eventually die under that of another—his own war. When Napoleon was only ten, his parents sent him off to a military academy near Paris. He devoted himself to studying the military tactics of the time, which eventually paid dividends when he was appointed, at age sixteen, to lieutenant in the artillery division. In less than eight years, he would make general. This was around the time that the revolution broke out in France, and he joined up with the French Revolutionary Army.

In late 1795, the government asked Napoleon to defend the palace that held the National Convention. He, along with a small army of men, overcame more than one thousand opponents in a matter of minutes. From that day, Napoleon was regarded as a French hero. With the current military directory in shambles, Napoleon saw his chance to lead and, in November 1799, staged a coup d'état in which five hundred of his soldiers took over a chamber of the national legislature and drove out the remaining members, leaving France to be governed by three consuls and naming Napoleon the first of these. These acts were followed by the creation of a plebiscite in which the citizens had the right to vote on issues with a simple yes or no. Four years later Napoleon would name himself emperor, even having the pope crown him. Many today recognize his coronation because of the famous painting by Jacques-Louis David that depicts it. Napoleon would again find himself in the middle of a war-driven state as the Third Coalition formed and brought war against France. In winning these wars, he would create the First French Empire. Eventually driven out of the empire by Russian tsar Alexander I, Napoleon died in exile on May 5, 1821.

Napoleon's biography here is deliberately brief because I believe that his reputation speaks for itself. He is one of the best-known conquerors and military commanders in history. So, what can we learn from him? The following section presents important "Napoleonic" thoughts about leadership and power.

"WHEN YOUR ENEMY IS EXECUTING A FALSE MOVEMENT, NEVER INTERRUPT HIM"

This quote, in various iterations, has been attributed to Napoleon, and whether he actually uttered the words, he certainly applied this philosophy to his wartime strategies. Napoleon recognized the need to understand an enemy's motivations, habits, and character, and like most wartime references, the advice can easily be applied to the business and social worlds. Make no mistake: Business is war. Life is war. Every day, someone wakes up with the same desire as you. Whether one of you achieves what you desire depends on how effectively you wage war against each other. Whether this "war" is actually violent is immaterial; it is still a contest in which the winner gets the spoils. Civil society and nature are not so different in their themes.

The term *enemy,* by modern interpretation, is not politically correct. We're supposed to help each other, to love each other, to support each other. But I don't see competition and collaboration (between "enemies") as mutually exclusive. I'm not talking about beating someone up, stealing, or committing crimes. I'm talking about beating others at whatever *game* you want to play, following that game's rules. If the game is business, then your enemies are everyone who wants the job that you want or the job that you have, and your goal is to do better, appear better, and sell yourself better to those who are hiring or buying. Your coworkers, even if they are your friends and family, are your enemy in the context of business. Think of playing a board game— you are playing with friends, but you are still playing to win. This might make them irritated with you if you win too much, and that quality is telling. If you are the type who plays to win and not for fun, and if you are the type who does not mind if your friend gets irritated and flips the board over afterward, you have a chance in the outside world. Many think "that guy" who plays to win is boorish, overly competitive. I disagree, and I think that sentiment comes more from jealousy than it does from a mere desire for a good time. Regardless, one can play to win during a game of Monopoly, and truly try one's hardest to undermine and sabotage and conquer the other players, while maintaining friendships afterward. Anyone who cannot do this, who cannot separate the two, is deadweight to you.

The term *enemy* generally refers to your competition. But there is also a more insidious enemy out there: you. Yes, *you* are also your own worst enemy. When you wake up in the morning to a buzzing alarm clock, what is the first thing you want to do more than anything? Most likely, it's to shut that noise off and go back to sleep. That's the enemy I'm speaking of. To know your enemy is to set two separate alarm clocks or, hell, to even put your alarm clock across the room so you can't just reach out and slam the snooze button. The heart of the lesson here is this: know yourself, know your weaknesses and your strengths, and you will be closer to obtaining the power you seek. You must learn to defeat your own weaknesses just as you would learn to take advantage of an enemy's weaknesses. This is because, as Napoleon says, someone out there is *waiting* for you to sleep in, to make that mistake, to lose your resolve.

When the enemy is your competition, things are more obvious. In our polite modern society, you can be friendly with your enemies, dine with them, socialize with them. In fact, if your enemy is currently embroiled in the field of study, or career, or social group you wish to conquer, then it behooves you to befriend your enemy as a strategy.

But that does not mean you are no longer enemies—your goal is still to best them as effectively as you can. Not all positions of power are mutually exclusive: sometimes there is room at the top for more than one person. But usually there is just one job opening, or one potential spouse, or one piece of cake. You want it, and so does your enemy. So, in spotting the pitfalls that you yourself may fall into, you should avoid them while simultaneously taking advantage of the fact that your enemy may *not* avoid them effectively. The alarm clock example is apt here: if *you* have trouble waking up in the morning, if it pains you to do it, odds are that it's hard for most everyone else as well. In that case, you should wake up *extra* early, get to work *that much earlier* than your fellows. Be the first to arrive *every time*. Sounds hard, doesn't it? Well, it sounds hard to your competition too, and therein lies your advantage. If you are *willing* to go that extra, difficult step, and your competition is not, then you have allowed them to make their own mistakes and you have filled the void they have left open with your presence.

Allowing someone else to make mistakes that you recognize is not necessarily sabotage—it is merely staying in your own lane, observing what doesn't work and avoiding those pitfalls yourself. It is every individual's prerogative to do this for themselves, and it is not anyone else's responsibility to coach you through any of life's "wars."

EDUCATE YOURSELF

I said it in the Machiavelli section, and I'll say it again now: read, read, read. There is a reason we constantly hear the old adage "Knowledge is power." Because it is true. Knowledge is your best weapon, your only advantage against any enemy or hardship. The more you know, the more power you can achieve. In Napoleon's words: "Read and meditate often about history: this is the only true philosophy . . . [R]ead and meditate about the wars of the Great Captains; that is the only way to study war." In the war of life, your mind is your weapon and knowledge is your ammo cache.

TRUE POWER IS EARNED, NOT INHERITED

Napoleon was one of, if not the earliest, champion of meritocracy in military ranking. "It was . . . most probably Napoleon himself, who brought the first truly modern military staff into existence," said George Nafziger, an American military historian, and this was due to Napoleon's consistent raging against the common practice at the time to poach the aristocracy to replenish the ranks of soldiers, simply because they were "noble." After 1800, under Napoleon's rule as premier consul, that began to change. Soldiers began to ascend purely based on their prowess in battle, not because of their nobility or their family ties. Today, in a democracy like America, we must remember that greatness can come from anywhere, no matter how humble the beginning. If you are assembling a team to help you achieve greatness, your only prejudice should be the abilities of your team members to get the job done—nothing more, nothing less. It does not matter if they are rich or poor, though being rich means access to resources, which helps. But a hardworking, talented impoverished person is more valuable than a lazy, incompetent rich person. Meritocracy is the name of the game, and after Napoleon put this into practice, he began to win battle after battle. The archaic world around him, much of which still believed in the concept of "noble blood," was likely flabbergasted as to why Napoleon's soldiers, captains, and generals were the best on earth. That is because Napoleon knew what you should know: that you only hire people who will get the job done, no matter where they come from.

IF YOU WANT IT DONE RIGHT, DO IT YOURSELF

Napoleon did not merely tell his soldiers when and where to fight; he went out there with them. While other monarchs were satisfied to sit in comfort behind palace walls, issuing orders through letters and middlemen, Napoleon was on the front lines. Because of this, he was better able to survey the battlefield, communicate his orders, and react expediently to changing circumstances. In addition to being practical, this hands-on approach is inspiring. Who would you rather work for, the boss who relaxes in Malibu all day and sends e-mails telling other people what to do, or the boss who, when he orders overtime, stays in the office with you and works just as hard, right alongside you? This is a way to court charisma: *We are all in this together, and I am your fearless leader.* If you wish to lead, be hands-on, lead from the thick of it, and you will likely find that people are more enthusiastic about following you and granting you power.

SPEAK WELL AND BE CONVINCING

Rhetoric is a powerful force. Someone who has been compelled by inspirational speech to *hope* can endure a lifetime of suffering and continue on. Certain winning presidential campaigns have been based entirely on the charismatic rhetoric of the candidate. Whether you are running a business, leading a country, or seeking power in a social group or a relationship, you must encourage those looking to you for answers. Otherwise, you will soon find them seeking other employment, or a new friend, or a new spouse. Without proper communication of ideas, there can be no productivity. Here, we see again a version of Machiavelli's precept on public opinion: it matters. If you can paint a picture with words and if people enjoy listening to you, they are more likely to grant you the power to accomplish what you need to accomplish. Your team at work has a deadline? Inspire them—your tenacity and your gung-ho attitude *are the reasons this will get done,* at least as far as they know. *Lead* your fellows into battle with your charisma and your enthusiasm and your words. Court the love and admiration of those around you, and pay close attention to how they respond to your efforts. So says Napoleon: "Public opinion is the thermometer a monarch should constantly consult."

For an example of someone who achieved power almost entirely from his manner of speaking and his monumental wit, we turn the clock forward . . .

WINSTON CHURCHILL

Success always demands a greater effort.

—Winston Churchill

Winston Churchill was born to an English lord and the daughter of an American millionaire, and despite a speech impediment (a reportedly excruciating lisp), he lived a relatively normal life for an English child in the late 1870s. Churchill spent most of his time in and out of boarding schools until he applied for and gained entrance in (after two failed attempts) the British Royal Military College.

The overcoming of an early disability is another quality seen in many successful leaders, and the telling and retelling of these stories is an important mental exercise. There will always be times, in this unfair world of ours, when you will feel as though the odds are stacked against you—because they *will* be stacked against you. But you will come to find that the majority of the great figures of history have been faced with very difficult obstacles initially, hence their greatness for overcoming them. Churchill's obstacle was his speech impediment, which he had to surmount not only to become the British prime minister, but to eventually become one of the most renowned speakers in all of history.

That *effort* in the face of truly unfair circumstances is the only thing standing between all of us and figures like Churchill. Yes, it was unfair that Churchill couldn't speak well. So what? He kept going and is now considered *the* prime example of rhetoric as inspirational and political tool. In Churchill's own words: "It is no use saying, 'We are doing our best.' You have got to succeed in doing what is necessary." How we feel about our circumstances—the asymmetries in our luck, our shortcomings, and the head starts of others—do not matter. Results are what matter.

From 1895 until 1899, Churchill served in the army, while also writing war correspondence for British newspapers. When he left the service, he continued his work as a war correspondent. While on the job, he was captured and kept as a prisoner in South Africa during the Second Boer War, until he eventually escaped. To do this, he traveled three hundred miles on his own, a feat for which he received a considerable amount of press. Once again, was there something inherent in him that allowed him to do this? By my lights, it was only tenacity, the unwillingness to give up, that made all of this possible. Which means it is possible for you too. Churchill would follow his tours of action and reporting with politics, becoming a member of the British Parliament in 1900. He became the president of the Board of Trade, then the First Lord of the Admiralty, modernizing Britain's naval fleet, then on to Secretary of State for War, for Air, and for the Colonies. Various controversies and political fragmentations in his party had Churchill defeated in the 1922 general election. He switched from the Labour Party to the Conservative Party, but he again met with defeat in the 1929 election.

He wrote books in the interim until the rise of Adolf Hitler, when Churchill became a vocal critic of the British government's conciliation with its rising Nazi neighbors. When news of German aggression against Norway viscerally illustrated Churchill's warnings and fears, he was quickly made prime minister under the authority of the Parliament and King George VI. Churchill went from being out of politics entirely, considered a right-wing extremist, to prime minister—all because he refused to hold his tongue, the very same tongue that caused him such inconvenience with its lisp. Think about that the next time you feel offended at someone for being "mean" or "controversial" on Twitter—maybe harsh public speech is a necessity, even if you don't agree with it.

Churchill was instrumental in first holding off the Nazis, as leader of the lone nation opposing them, and then establishing relationships with the United States and the other Allied powers. After 1942, the tides began to turn. With President Franklin Roosevelt now on board, the war was eventually won, and Churchill took a leadership position afterward, helping establish the United Nations as a new hub for international affairs. Later on, Churchill gave his famous "The Sinews of Peace" speech (also known as the "Iron Curtain" speech) in the United States, effectively drawing up the battle lines of the Cold War against what was recently an ally, the Soviet Union.

Churchill's greatest weakness early in life, his ability to speak, became his greatest strength later, no doubt due to diligent training and education. He will be remembered as many things to many people, but even his enemies acknowledged that his wit as an orator was indisputable. As Churchill said himself, in an unpublished essay entitled "The Scaffolding of Rhetoric": "Of all the talents bestowed upon men, none is so precious as the gift of oratory. He who enjoys it wields a power more durable than that of a great king." In business and life, these words are true—almost nothing is more important than being able to clearly and passionately communicate. You will find the better you speak, the more you are listened to. Starting to see a pattern here, aren't we?

The fact that he was often vilified meant Churchill's job wasn't the easiest. On October 29, 1941, when World War II was raging, in an address to the students at Harrow School, Churchill strengthened the resolve of his people by evoking his iron will to carry on: "Never give in, never give in, never, never, never, never—in nothing, great or small, large or petty—never give in except to convictions of honour and good sense." From his earliest endeavors, including escaping as a POW and traveling three hundred miles to Mozambique, Churchill lived this maxim to the letter, most clearly seen in his stern hand in governing. As many people vilify Churchill as admire him still today, as it is with most politicians. Many, in fact, may come to criticize *you,* once you step into the ring. When the critics inevitably come for you, once you have made your bed and are obliged to lie in it, remember what Churchill's fellow iconoclast Teddy Roosevelt said in his 1910 speech "Citizenship in a Republic," delivered at the Sorbonne:

It is not the critic who counts; not the man who points out how the strong man stumbles, or where the doer of deeds could have done them better. The credit belongs to the man who is actually in the arena, whose face is marred by dust and sweat and blood; who strives valiantly; who errs, who comes short again and again, because there is no effort without error and shortcoming; but who does actually strive to do the deeds; who knows great enthusiasms, the great devotions; who spends himself in a worthy cause; who at the best knows in the end the triumph of high achievement, and who at the worst, if he fails, at least fails while daring greatly, so that his place shall never be with those cold and timid souls who neither know victory nor defeat.

If that doesn't convince you, try Churchill's own words: "You will never get to the end of the journey if you stop to shy a stone at every dog that barks."

You may be hated, criticized, and shunned by people for making hard decisions in the pursuit of a singular goal. This is part of the game. When he made his "Iron Curtain" speech, Churchill was railing against the expansion of the Soviet Union, which only a few years before had been an ally of Britain and the United States in the war against Germany. Churchill did not hesitate to lambast his former ally as a growing threat—and for good reason. If you are in a partnership with your best friend and have a workforce of a thousand, and your partner commits an act that could put the company under—putting those people out of a job—you must be resolute. Your partner, your friend, *must go*. No matter how friendly the two of you are. No matter if you grew up considering this person a brother or sister. This is a pragmatic decision—a consequentialist decision and, indeed, a *Machiavellian* decision—in its purest form. Churchill faced this type of decision on a massive scale—not in the context of friends and business partners, but allied nations.

In situations such as the one I've just described, many business owners would sit around twiddling their thumbs and hoping their partner's mistake was a one-time accident that could be forgiven. Their loyalties, they say, lie with their friends, even if their friends are hurting the livelihoods of innocent people who rely on them for work. You know what I say? *No*. That's not a chance I would be willing to take. And I *have* had to make this decision, more than once, with people I would otherwise consider as close as family. For my part, I don't actually have many friends, and I don't mind it. I have my family, of course, and I have my associates, my bandmates, my partners who are effective leaders themselves—they are my friends, and they understand my mentality because they possess it as well.

But, in the past, if my friends threatened the livelihood of my business, my dreams, or my goals, I made the sacrifice: I fired my friends. You too may have to do the same. Your friends are your future, and if your friends hold you back or come into conflict with your greater goal, you must be prepared to make a sacrifice.

It is easy to judge from the outside, but step into the arena with me—see what you are made of, and you may find that decisions people in power make that seem callous are actually necessary for the greater good: the goal, the goal, the goal. As Churchill put it in his very first speech as prime minister, delivered in May 1940: "You ask, what is our aim? I can answer in one word: Victory—victory at all costs, victory in spite of all terror, victory, however long and hard the road may be; for without victory, there is no survival."

MODERN POWER PLAYERS

**It is not the strongest of the species that
survives, nor the most intelligent; it is
the one most adaptable to change.**

—Attributed to various sources, derived from
Charles Darwin's *On the Origin of Species*

We live in a world that's faster paced than
Machiavelli's, or Napoleon's, or Churchill's.
Never before have people ascended to millionaire and billionaire status as quickly from
nothing, become global celebrities with little to no dis-
cernible talent, and risen to political power without
the traditional bona fides to back them up. We have
also never before seen a public so eager to tear down
those who do ascend. Regardless of whether you morally agree or disagree with this new model, you picked
up this book because you want to understand power,
and likely because you want to seize it for yourself.

Whether you approve of the decisions made by the figures in this book, you must acknowledge that they succeeded in seizing power using whatever it took, despite their weaknesses. What they did with their power after that, and whether we judge their actions to be ethical, are for another book.

Power today carries a steep learning curve, and it gets steeper by the day. You will enter the workforce expecting to be the master of your own ship. But Mother Nature will send hurricanes and tidal waves to thwart you. When the storm comes, you must adapt. You must bring the sail down; you must brace yourself. In other words: you must react in accordance with the reality in which you live. Planting your feet stubbornly is not always the best strategy.

In order to do this most effectively, we must look to those who have navigated rough waters successfully and try to determine why they made certain maneuvers and how they did them.

Why does Warren Buffett attend ribbon-cutting ceremonies for furniture stores he holds a stake in when he could sit back and relax as a billionaire seventy times over?

Why did Michael Jordan practice like his life depended on it well into his thirties, when he had already won multiple championships, and why did he work so hard to become a shoe and fashion entrepreneur and achieve billionaire status, when he could have just sat back on his athletic millions and lived like a king?

Why are Elon Musk and Jeff Bezos now in the space travel business, when they've already made billions on the ground?

Why does Oprah Winfrey continue to launch new ventures, like her magazine and her TV network, when she is already one of the richest women in the world?

These individuals are like sharks, circling the waters of opportunity. They love the game itself, the conquest. The truly powerful are different because they love the process, the hunt, as much as they love the rewards. To keep up with the other sharks, they must keep moving or they might lose out on a big catch. Whatever their individual motivations, this life philosophy of constant improvement, of always more, of always bigger and better, is what unites them.

With that said, let's explore a few examples of what it means to become powerful in the modern era.

OPRAH WINFREY

THE QUEEN

What I learned at a very young age was that I was responsible for my life . . . You cannot blame apartheid, your parents, your circumstances, because you are not your circumstances. You are your possibilities. If you know that, you can do anything.
—Oprah Winfrey

In terms of contrast between early life and current situation, perhaps no figure mentioned in this book is as impressive as Oprah Winfrey. Born to a single, teenaged mother, she was raised partially by her grandmother, who was so poor that Winfrey often had to wear potato sacks for clothing, for which she was relentlessly teased. Adding injury to insult, her grandmother would often cane her when she felt the young Winfrey was out of line. Winfrey would later reveal to the world that a cousin, an uncle, and another individual had repeatedly molested her as a child, which she cited as the reason she ran away from home in her early teens. She would subsequently become pregnant with a son at age fourteen, who was born prematurely and died.

Winfrey's early hardships in life seemed endless, from an absentee father to sexual abuse. Despite all of this, she became an honors student, earning a scholarship to Tennessee State University, and even won a beauty pageant. She eventually landed her first broadcasting job at a local radio station.

Before we continue, it bears noticing that the nar-

rative arc of Winfrey's life would already be extraor-
dinary if she had stopped there. It is rare that life gets
much harder than Winfrey's was up until her early
twenties, and rarer still for someone to emerge from
the mire with direction, drive, and purpose. She went
through hell and kept going. It's corny, but it also gives
one perspective: if she can get through what she did,
then you can get through your (probably much lesser)
hardships.

Winfrey eventually began hosting her first talk
show, *People Are Talking,* and eight years later she
took over another struggling show, called *A.M. Chicago,* which upon her arrival became a major success
and the #1-rated talk show in the country. Her fame
brought her to the attention of Steven Spielberg, who
cast Winfrey in his movie *The Color Purple,* a role for
which Winfrey earned an Oscar nomination. After
that, it looked as though nothing could stop her. Soon
came the now-famous *Oprah Winfrey Show,* and the
rest is history—she was soon a global phenomenon,
with her show broadcast in more than one hundred
countries. Originally criticized for being sensational-
ist, she rebranded her show with a new focus on self-
improvement and spirituality, and launched her cultlike
Oprah's Book Club, with nearly every selection, known
and unknown, being immediately catapulted to the top
of the bestseller list. She also began doing high-profile
celebrity interviews, launched Harpo Productions, and
created the magazine *O.* More recently, she ended her
talk show and launched her own television network,
the Oprah Winfrey Network.

Winfrey is, perhaps, the best example on this list of someone with power who is bolstered by, but not necessarily dependent on, her money. More valuable than her funds is her *brand* (a brand so recognizable one need mention only her first name) and her relationship with a teeming mass of rabid fans who hang on her every word and recommendation as gospel. I am not the first to call her one of the most influential women on the planet. For three years, she was the world's only black billionaire. She has affected public policy—President Bill Clinton signed a bill creating a database of convicted child abusers that she initially proposed to Congress—and she received the Presidential Medal of Freedom from President Barack Obama in 2013, the highest honor possible for a civilian, and the Bob Hope Humanitarian Award before that, for her almost uncountable number of philanthropic ventures. By some measures she is the most highly accomplished black philanthropist of all time. All of these honors and recognitions contribute to her power—the power to make large-scale changes that can influence the lives of potentially millions of people.

What is the most useful tool in Winfrey's arsenal? In my view, there are two: her charisma and her endurance. Without charisma, how could she have taken a low-rated, virtually unknown talk show and made it #1, and from there move on to create a media empire? To a certain degree, charisma is innate—we are who we are, and we are as likable as we are. However, there are niches one can tap in to if one is honest about what one brings to the table. For Oprah Winfrey, it was her frankness, wit, and air of trustworthiness and compassion that seemed to connect with her guests and viewers on a deep level. She was, likely, creating the show that she always wanted to see and never quite got from the tabloid TV that existed before her. And when it comes to her second crucial Power Tool, like Churchill's, Winfrey's was one of utter endurance. Neither ever gave up, no matter how bleak the circumstances seemed.

ELON MUSK

I feel fear quite strongly so it's not that I don't have fear. But if I think it's important enough then I just override the fear.
—Elon Musk

For Elon Musk, the South African–born billionaire known for entrepreneurial ventures such as Zip2, Pay-Pal, Tesla, and SpaceX, the crucial moment to seize power came in 1992, when he was still a college student at Queen's University in Ontario. The Internet was brand new at this time, and its potential infinite. Elon was living in Canada when the boom began, and he knew where he wanted to go: America. So he transferred to the University of Pennsylvania, where he would ultimately end up receiving two degrees: a bachelor of science in physics and a bachelor of science in economics. Elon wanted to be where the action was—Silicon Valley—and he would eventually get even closer, but more on that later.

What was Elon's initial power move? Was it the leap of faith he took when he initially decided to move to America? Maybe it was. Sometimes that initial leap of faith is the most important decision you will ever make. Martin Luther King Jr. once said, "Faith is taking the first step even when you can't see the whole staircase." While I espouse preparation and education, I firmly believe that taking a leap of faith will be necessary at certain crucial junctures in your journey toward power.

When asked about the secrets of his success, Elon has cited the importance of networking and, in particular, cold-calling. When Elon was still a student in Canada, he was looking for a job one summer and read in the newspaper about Peter Nicholson, then the head of the Bank of Nova Scotia, who he thought sounded really smart and interesting. Elon had no connection to Nicholson, but he tracked down his number and called him directly, eventually persuading Nicholson to hire him for a summer internship. Talk about a shot in the dark. I have people come to me all the time with ideas just like this, and I'm usually willing to hear them out. Sometimes that's exactly what it takes.

Machiavelli stated in *The Prince,* "The first method for estimating the intelligence of a ruler is to look at the men he has around him." Well, what better way to gather people of intelligence around you than to cold-call them and ask for their advice? I'm not suggesting you find my number and call my house (in fact, please don't). But if you find a way to seize my ear with something that catches my attention, I'm open to a conversation—always. It is up to you to hook me, or whomever else you may be considering, with a good idea and with yourself. That first brave step of cold-calling a stranger speaks to Musk's character—he is a *doer,* in situations where other people would have faltered for fear of offending, or being perceived as rude or presumptuous. Do not fear being presumptuous. Presume. Presume you are going to achieve greatness.

With his two degrees from the University of Pennsylvania under his belt, Musk headed to Stanford University to enroll in a Ph.D. program but dropped out two days later. The Internet boom was now exploding, and he wanted to pursue entrepreneurial ventures. With a $28,000 loan from their father, Elon and his brother, Kimbal, started a company called Zip2, which marketed "city search" software to online newspapers. They made deals with the *Chicago Tribune* and the *New York Times,* which both began using the program for their online subscribers. Four years later the brothers sold the company for $307 million. What is the lesson here? Is it that graduate school is a waste of time? Clearly that's not the point. The lesson is, simply, that the *timing* of an act is just as important as the act itself. Musk was paying attention to the world around him, and when he saw a pattern emerging, he was quick to capitalize on it. In any situation, business or personal, this hyperawareness and sense of timing are crucial.

Just before the turn of the millennium, Musk would use his momentum to form another company, X.com, which would eventually become PayPal, later acquired by eBay for $1.5 billion. Musk has gone from gamble to gamble, using much of his profits from his previous successes to fund his next ventures. He formed SpaceX *the same year* eBay acquired PayPal. So far, it seems to be paying off. SpaceX makes headlines regularly, becoming the first private company to send commercial spacecraft up to the International Space Station.

Achieving excellence in one field will often open up opportunities in other fields (and provide you with the *power*—that is, the dollars—to fund these subsequent opportunities). There are different ways to do this. I, personally, play *safe bets,* and it's always worked for me. I have backup plans on top of backup plans, I never gamble, and I almost never volunteer my own personal funds if I can simply sell an idea instead. Musk is more of a thrill-seeker. He tends to put all his eggs in one basket when he launches a new project, and more often than not, his gambles pay off. You can go with either approach—the choice is yours. In the end, your results are what matter. You must be the judge, deciding for yourself which risks are reasonable to take and then bearing the responsibility for your decisions.

Behold the birth of Tesla and the first electric sports car, released in 2008. At the time, this was a very *high-risk* gamble. But the thing about high risk is, of course, that the rewards are high. Tesla is now a trailblazer in energy-efficient automobiles with revenues of billions of dollars per year. In fact, Tesla's power cannot be measured in just dollars, but also in its influence over older and much more established carmakers like BMW and Mercedes-Benz, who are now under pressure to produce energy-efficient and electric cars of their own in order to compete with Tesla.

Musk has no illusions about the riskiness of his key moves in the past; he has said publicly, "Failure is an option here. If things are not failing, you are not in-novating enough," and, referencing a SpaceX launch in 2012, "I feel very lucky." What Musk cannot control are twists of fate. What he can control are the risks he is willing to take and the consequences he is willing to deal with if he *fails.* Failure is at the forefront of his mind, and if you are dealing with the real world in any way, you will have to deal with it. Musk may fail in the future. It seems that he is only getting started. But if you watch his TED Talk and pay attention to his public statements over the years, you will notice that he is transparent about the risks and the personal cost he is willing to shoulder.

If you have the guts to put it all on the line, and if you are willing to fail over and over again, to risk losing everything you have, then perhaps the thrill-seeker strategy is for you. I, personally, like the slow and steady route, but hey, the choice is yours. We shall see how Musk's ventures play out when the Hyperloop transportation system he unveiled plans for in 2013 finally comes to fruition. It might not be for another decade . . . or two. Patience: another quality to learn from Musk.

DAVE GROHL

NOT ALL ROCK STARS ARE DUMB!
(JUST MOST OF 'EM)

I honestly believe that if you're focused and passionate and driven, you can achieve anything you want to achieve in life. I honestly believe that. Because you'll fucking figure it out . . . I never took lessons to play . . . I just figured it out . . . But I would listen and practice by myself in my bedroom obsessively. And so throughout life I've always kind of figured that that's just how you do stuff.
—Dave Grohl

Lest you think I'm the only self-motivated rock guy out there who has made it, but who continues to treat each day as if it's the only chance in life he'll get, let me introduce you to someone who shares my attitude: Dave Grohl. Grohl is a writer, musician, and producer. He was the drummer in Nirvana and now leads his own band, Foo Fighters. We've met and spoken briefly a number of times, but mostly, I have observed him from afar. In the world of self-destructive, drug-infested rock stardom, he seems to be the exception to the rule. More so than many of his contemporaries (and mine, for that matter), his *work ethic* makes him stand out.

So many of my fellow musicians are, pardon the expression, *bums*. They are merely *lucky* that their music took off, because without it, they would have no recourse in the real world and would likely still be in their parents' basements. I've seen people ascend to the status of international icon, only to blow every last cent on trivialities and break up their bands over relationships, drugs, and ego.

If KISS had not taken off, I might still be a teacher in New York City, and proud of it. Or I might be doing something different. My point is I would be doing something, and I would be doing it successfully. I would have found a way, because that's what I've always done. I've always had a plan B and a plan C, because I know that life is not fair, and when reality takes everything away from you, you must be ready to start all over again.

This is the mentality that Dave Grohl shares. When Grohl was a kid, he was restless and aimless, a high school dropout. He was, it seems, aware of these shortcomings. But he loved music, loved it with a *passion,* and he found that he could pour all his energy into music and never get sick of it. There is something to be learned here, and it is something Grohl has said that can apply to any vocation: "You will only be great at things you love to do."

This is key to power. When we look at people who have achieved excellence in a certain field, these are not people who chose their field haphazardly or due to peer pressure. Whatever industry these people are in, they're doing it because they loved it. They also practiced and worked at what they do. *All day long.* They did not take breaks. They did not take vacations.

They did not get tired of it. Because when you love

what you do, you won't tire of it. You will get more done, and you will do it better and faster. If Grohl had pursued marine biology instead of music, most likely he would not have achieved greatness, because he wouldn't have loved what he was doing. It would have felt like work, he would have wanted to take breaks, and vacations and breaks are a waste of time. Passionate work stimulates the mind like a car engine recharges its battery—by running, not by resting. The actress Helen Hayes said it best: "If you rest, you rust." Find something you never have to take a break from, and you will find your path to power.

And in the meantime, there is no shame in taking a day job. But your time off from your day job should not be spent sitting around and watching TV. Your free time should be spent pursuing your passion, the job you *actually* want to be doing. "I was in the same fucking position you are in twenty fucking years ago. That was it. I worked at a fucking furniture warehouse and I wanted people to like my music, so I played out as much as I could. If you're passionate and driven and focused at what you do, and if you're really fucking good at it, people are gonna take notice," says Grohl.

From the time he was seventeen, Grohl was in and out of bands. He followed his favorites and befriended them, including the Melvins, who eventually introduced him to Kurt Cobain and Krist Novoselic. Again, here is that lesson I've talked about over and over again: hang out with people who are doing what you want to be doing. *Show me your friends and I'll show you your future.* Grohl knew that the Melvins were doing what he wanted to be doing, so he found a way in and made friends. Whether he did this consciously, as a strategy of professional networking, his nose pointed always toward what he loved doing and toward those who were doing what he loved doing. This led him directly into the company of what would eventually become one of the biggest bands of their era: Nirvana.

Then came the true test of Grohl's work ethic. What happens after you achieve success and it is torn from you? Life happens. Even if you follow the advice in this book to the letter and achieve success, life happens and bad things happen, because the world is not fair. Grohl was riding a cresting wave of success before Cobain died. In the aftermath of Cobain's suicide, Grohl found himself without a best friend and without direction. Among the trauma and the devastation, he was also suddenly without a band, a free agent. I think it is safe to say that the normal response to this would be early retirement—he had achieved something very few attain, after all, and now it was over. What were the odds he could do it again without his front man?

But as we know, this is not the end of Grohl's story, because Grohl loves music, he loves playing and recording and *working at it* every single day. He is the type who cannot sit still for even a moment without picking up an instrument, without *doing*. He could have relaxed after Nirvana, luxuriated on a secure legacy as a member of a band that changed the face of music. But he decided to do the hardest thing in the world when you've reached the pinnacle of success:

Start over.

Do it again.

Make a name for yourself *again*—a brand-new name.

As Grohl put it, in a 2016 interview with the web series *Off Camera with Sam Jones*:

> When Kurt died, I woke up the next day and thought, "I'm lucky to be alive." So much that still, to this day, I feel that every morning when I wake up, because it's so strange to think that person was just here and now they're gone. And I'm still here? And maybe tomorrow I could be gone as well? It was a profound revelation I had the day after he died and it changed everything. It honestly changed so much of my life that I felt the most important thing was just appreciating being alive, good day or bad day. But after Kurt died, I really felt that way, like, "Okay, I'm gonna try this. What do I have to lose? I'm gonna start this band and then I'm gonna be the singer."

Something my mother always said to me as a child: "Every day above ground is a good day." Notice a pattern here?

For the first Foo Fighters album, not only did Grohl front the band and sing—he *played every instrument on the record*. Drums, bass, guitar. Everything. Musicians get a lot of flak for being lazy bums. And most of us are. But not this one. Whether he is willing to admit it, Grohl is an entrepreneur. Grohl gets up and *works* every day, and makes things happen, with his bare hands if he must. By a few different counts—live ticket sales, record sales—Foo Fighters is now an even *bigger band* than Nirvana ever was, and longer running. They have eight albums behind them, with thirty million records sold worldwide and counting, and a documentary series called *Sonic Highways* on HBO, in which a song is written for each episode, inspired by the city they are in (the show became the genesis of an ambitious concept album). The list goes on, and this impressive scorecard can be laid directly at the feet of good old-fashioned *labor of love.*

Whether your industry is making shoes, data crunching, running a restaurant, or anything else, there is much to be gleaned from Grohl's work ethic and strategy. He even toured the world with his band with a *broken leg,* bound to a chair he had constructed out of recycled guitar necks, like some rock-opera *Game of Thrones.* The actual accident occurred during a concert in Gothenburg, Sweden, in 2015, when Grohl fell off the stage. He announced over the mic that drummer Taylor Hawkins would lead the band and cover some of the songs while he was rushed to the hospital. But before he was carted off in an ambulance, he promised the audience that he would be back to finish the show. Hawkins carried on, and Grohl *returned an hour later* and proceed to play a further two-hour set, perched on a chair with a fresh cast on his leg.

This is yet another situation in which it would have been totally understandable to just *take some time off,* to *rest,* to *rust,* like any normal person would, like the doctor probably ordered. But not Grohl. This story is a microcosm for Grohl's life and work ethic. He is someone who seems incapable of sitting still, of stopping, of giving up. What kind of person doesn't take time off, even for injury and hospitalization? The kind who loves what he does. The kind whose vacation *is* his work. The kind who succeeds. The kind who seizes power and lives by his own terms. This is what separates the powerful from the rest, in any field. Never take vacations. Never take breaks. Unless I am absolutely bedridden, I work every day. Life is work, and if your work is something you love, it will never feel like work.

One more lesson from Grohl, a quote from a 2014 interview he gave to the *Guardian*, which needs very little explanation from me: "You don't need a needle hanging out of your arm to be a rock star."

Amen to that.

MICHAEL JORDAN

THE LEGEND

I've missed over nine thousand shots in my career. I've lost almost three hundred games. Twenty-six times I've been trusted to take the game-winning shot . . . and missed. I've failed over and over and over again in my life. And that is why I succeed.
—Michael Jordan

Michael Jordan's name is synonymous with basketball, winning, and shoes. He's a five-time NBA MVP with six NBA championships, who has earned more than $93 million over the course of his basketball career. But all of that pales in comparison to the entrepreneurial titan and businessman extraordinaire that he has become since retiring from the NBA. In 2014, *Forbes* estimated that Michael Jordan takes in more than $100 million a year from Nike and other partners.

Michael Jeffrey Jordan was born in 1963 in Brooklyn, New York. His parents were working class, and soon after his birth, they moved their family of six to Wilmington, North Carolina. At a young age, Michael was said to have been massively competitive, not just with others but also with himself. This competitive drive would push him to outperform all others on the basketball court. Despite this, in 1978 as a high school sophomore, he tried out for his school's varsity basketball team, and he *failed*. Standing at only five foot ten at the time, Jordan was not a standout on the court. He was one of fifty students who attempted to make the fifteen-member roster. Once the team list was posted on the wall of the gym, Jordan searched for his name that wasn't there. He then went home, locked himself in his bedroom, and cried.

Many people at this point would have given up. You've been rejected—it's over. But the decision you make when you arrive at that fork in the road determines your fate and your future.

"Whenever I was working out and got tired and figured I ought to stop, I'd close my eyes and see that list in the locker room without my name on it," Jordan has said. He turned the disappointment of not making the varsity team into fuel, and he lit a fire that would last a lifetime. He committed to training and to getting better. And though he didn't make the varsity team, he would go on to earn a spot on the JV squad. His performance that season, I imagine, was one that the varsity coach would not soon forget. Jordan scored multiple forty-point games on JV. He grew four inches and he easily made the varsity team his junior year, going on to become their leading scorer, averaging more than twenty points per game.

Despite becoming a starting varsity player, Jordan's work ethic only increased in intensity. He was constantly in the gym lifting weights and running drills. Countless hours led to his standout senior year, where Jordan would average a triple-double (that's an average of double figures in at least three categories—in Jordan's case points, assists, and rebounds—which I'm told is a big deal). He was an All-American and a top recruit at nearly all the major college basketball programs. Eventually signing to play for the University of North Carolina, Jordan would thrive in the college setting and lead his team to the NCAA championship game, scoring the buzzer-beating game-winner. Jordan then left UNC after his junior season to enter his name into the NBA Draft.

In this new arena, Jordan would be undervalued yet again. He was passed on by the Houston Rockets and the Portland Trailblazers, at the first and second pick, ending up on the Chicago Bulls at the third overall spot in the 1984 NBA Draft. Interesting to note that Jordan made the time in his busy NBA schedule to return to North Carolina and finish his degree in geography. The rest, if you have a sports inclination, is a matter of celebrated record: six NBA championships, six-time NBA Finals MVP, five-time NBA MVP, fourteen NBA All-Star teams, three-time NBA All-Star MVP, ten All-NBA First Team honors, 1988 NBA Defensive Player of the Year, ten-time NBA Scoring Champion, three-time NBA Steals Leader, two-time NBA Slam Dunk Contest champion, and three-time Associated Press Athlete of the Year, along with a litany of other awards too numerous to list.

Jordan spent the end of his playing career learning the ins and outs of basketball operations. He worked with the front office before and during his tenure on the court with the Washington Wizards and in 2006 purchased a stake in the newly established Charlotte Bobcats (now the Charlotte Hornets). Soon after, Jordan took his love for the game of basketball and applied it to the basketball operations off the court. Jordan had been a rich man before, but once he purchased an even larger stake in the team in 2010 and the Charlotte Bobcats were reevaluated financially, he reached billionaire status. Jordan found something he loves and refuses to quit it, even after his on-court experience was over.

The other half of Jordan's business is shoes. Following his college career, Jordan signed a contract with sports agent David Falk. The first order of business was a shoe contract like all the other top-tier players of the time had. What Falk and Jordan didn't know was that Nike already had its sights set on making Jordan the new face of Nike basketball. When the Air Jordan brand launched, it was projected to make $3 million in its first year of sales alone, but instead it ended up making $130 million for Nike, proving to be the most successful sports endorsement relationship in history. This relationship would continue into the 1990s, creating a buzz for the prized shoes. The more limited the quantities, the higher the demand, resulting in camped-out customers outside shoe stores and occasional riots—all due to the brand of Jordan himself, the image he cultivated with his success and his work ethic. His name became synonymous with greatness. The Nike Jordan brand commanded $2.6 billion in shoes alone, and another $1 billion in apparel and international business, per a 2015 *Forbes* report.

Think back to Jordan's first rejection, when he failed to make the varsity basketball team and stood staring at that list in the locker room without his name on it. Hold that image in your mind, just like Jordan did. The next time you find yourself being blocked from achieving your dreams by something external, call up that image like Jordan did and use it as fuel. Commit to working harder and to getting even better. Never stop.

If you take this to heart, you will be that much closer to power.

STAN LEE

THE CREATOR

I learned early on that I'm not that different from most other people. So if I can come up with a character I think is exciting . . . I figure a lot of people maybe will have the same taste I do.
—Stan Lee

Stan Lee is a machine. He is best known for his work at Marvel Comics as the cocreator of legendary comic-book characters who now hold dominion over the global movie box office. He's also that funny guy who makes a cameo in every Marvel film. Lee, like most other examples of powerful people in this book, had humble beginnings. But in his story, you will see a pattern that you should take to heart. The "Marvel Method" is not simply the way Lee crafted stories with his paneling and inking team. It is an unstoppable ethic that makes his work indistinguishable from his life.

Born in the Bronx in 1922, Lee took on tons (and *tons*) of odd jobs as a young kid growing up, everything from delivering sandwiches for the pharmacy at Rockefeller Center, to selling *New York Herald Tribune* subscriptions door-to-door, to writing obituaries, to working as an usher at a Broadway theater. Another lesson to be learned: No job is beneath you, especially when you're starting out.

Young people today seem to grow up with a sense of entitlement and the idea that making someone's coffee, fetching someone's dry cleaning, or working at a drive-through is embarrassing. This attitude must be snuffed out. And the best way to do that is to cite the myriad heroes of today who were once the unpaid interns, errand boys, and coffee-makers of yesterday. You should approach every job you have with gratitude that anyone wants to pay you to do *anything at all*. Approaching even the crudest, most servile jobs with enthusiasm, and a drive to not only complete your tasks but to *excel* in them, is the only way to ascend the first crucial steps on your ladder to power. If Stan Lee did it, you have no right to feel "above it." Get to work.

Lee graduated early from high school, at the age of sixteen, and set out to become a serious writer. Stan Lee began as a pseudonym (his real name was Stanley Martin Lieber) that he would later adopt as his legal name. As I did, and as many other modern power players have done, Lee used his name to reinvent himself and to create a persona. You may want to consider doing the same, especially if your name is long or hard to pronounce. Remember, if you want people to grant you power, they'll need to remember your name upon first hearing it. There is power in simplicity, and there is power in being memorable.

In 1939, Lee's uncle, Robbie Solomon, helped him get a job as an assistant at a company called Timely Comics, which would, much later, become Marvel. Yet another lesson here: Accepting help from those who can hold doors open for you is nothing to be ashamed of. You are in this to succeed, and that's what networking is all about. If you know someone who knows someone, use that connection. In this first job for Timely Comics, Lee was initially assigned to menial tasks, like refilling ink for the artists and getting lunch and coffee. His proficiency in these tasks impressed people and eventually led to him being allowed to try his hand at filling in text, and ultimately, he was made an editor and began creating characters. The only way to make that leap like Lee did, from underling to editor, is with good old-fashioned hard labor and enthusiasm. People will notice you if you do your job, whatever job it may be, better than anyone else around you. If you are just starting out, strive to be the best at getting coffee, and make your dreams for the future known as you are doing it. Soon, you may ingratiate yourself with the right person, and that person may give you the opportunity to not get coffee anymore. This is the old model of climbing the ladder, and it still works.

Lee left the company in 1942 to serve in the army, and once he returned, he had to do some work to reestablish himself. Remember: success is not a straight line. He struggled for a while and considered changing careers and giving up his dream. But eventually, with artist Jack Kirby, he created his first superhero team, the Fantastic Four. And from there he would go on to cocreate characters that are now known to almost everyone on the planet, nerd or not: the X-Men, the Avengers, including the Hulk, Iron Man, Spider-Man, and Doctor Strange. He wrote these characters for a time, then graduated to full-time publisher at Marvel, passing the torch to other artists and storytellers who carry on his characters' stories to this day, on the page and on screen.

Lee is credited with creating the first African American superhero, Falcon, who appears in an issue of *Captain America*. He would go on to use his series, including *Spider-Man*, to tackle deeper human issues than his contemporaries had done, including the dangers of drug use, discrimination, and racism, and subsequently the rest of the industry followed suit, loosening censorship codes to allow for the discussion of darker real-world issues. The lesson here: If you want to make a tangible difference in the world, it is necessary to have the *power* to do so. In Lee's case, that power meant having the megaphone to get these positive social messages out into the world, via the ascension and popularity of his characters.

Marvel as a company got into financial trouble in the nineties and began selling its most popular characters to movie studios to make ends meet. The firm filed for bankruptcy in 1997, and it looked as if collapse was inevitable. However, at the turn of the millennium, Marvel began partnering with Twentieth Century Fox to produce a series of successful film franchises, including the X-Men and Spider-Man movies, which were smash hits. The strength of Marvel, and what allowed the company to emerge from bankruptcy and survive, was due to Lee's original characters. Today, Marvel owns some of the most popular and lucrative film franchises in the world.

Lee was awarded a National Medal of the Arts from Congress in 2008. Now, you suppose, comes the time when Lee can sit back and enjoy his secure legacy. Not likely. Lee still writes books, cocreates characters, produces TV shows, and makes a cameo in almost every single Marvel movie. He even makes regular appearances at comic conventions. In a 2014 interview he gave to the *Chicago Tribune,* he said, "I don't have to do them, but I like being with the fans. I learn more from them than they learn from me." It is safe to say that he will likely never retire while he can stand on two legs. He could rest. Most people in his position would. But he won't—he doesn't want to. At the age of *ninety-four,* there is still *more* to be done.

There go all of your excuses: You're tired. You're getting *too old* for this. The true renaissance of Lee's creations is, arguably, happening *right now.* It is my opinion that this would not be the case without his work ethic and the ethic of his successors who learned from him.

Take note of this attitude: the goal of Lee's work was not to earn enough to rest or retire. The goal of Lee's work has always been to keep moving and to keep creating. Perpetual motion is the name of the game.

WARREN BUFFETT

THE SOOTHSAYER

Someone's sitting in the shade today because someone planted a tree a long time ago.
—Warren Buffett

Not all powerful people are mean-spirited in the pursuit of their ambitions. There is a gray area between aggressive, victory-oriented behavior and malicious behavior, and the man who walks that line best, by my lights, is Warren Buffett. He is, by all accounts, a decent man with a high moral compass. He makes headlines for being one of the few mega-billionaires with a reputation for his absolutely fair, compassionate, and by-the-books business practices. Though he aggressively pursues his goals, he seems to do so without earning anyone's particular ire. For Buffett, being an ethical operator is not just a principled decision; it is a pragmatic decision. Buffett has said, "It's easier to stay out of trouble than it is to get out of trouble." And I agree. Even if you take my advice about being Machiavellian to heart, you will realize that breaking the law, screwing people over needlessly, lying, and cheating are not worth the risk to your own personal fortune and goals. Choosing to be honest, trustworthy, and charitable is not a moral decision. It is a *pragmatic,* calculated decision, because you want to be as safe as possible and to protect your interests. When people know that they can trust you, there's power in that.

Buffett was born in 1930 in Omaha, Nebraska. His father started his own investment company when Warren was just a child and worked diligently through the aftermath of the stock market crash. At the age of eight, Buffett picked up a book called *One Thousand Ways to Make $1000,* by F. C. Minaker. Inspired and hoping to increase his nickel-a-week allowance, he sold Coca-Cola, gum, and magazines door-to-door. From these humble but ambitious beginnings, Buffett would go on to become the only person to create a top-ten Fortune 500 company from the ground up.

Entrepreneurship can provide spiritual moments in a young person's life. This is how I feel about my experiences scrubbing fat off a butcher's chopping block and delivering newspapers as a kid. These things changed me internally and have shaped who I am today. I imagine Buffett learned the same thing I learned: it feels *good* when nobody is there to tell you what to do. In other words, he liked being his own boss. Even in modest circumstances, if you are willing to put in the hours and be clever about what people around you need, you can have the power to be your own boss. Once again, so long as you do not consider a certain job "beneath you." That sort of ego is your enemy, especially starting out.

Warren's father never cared much about money. He lived according to an inner scorecard and didn't pay attention to what other people had. He would go on to run for Congress, and to win, but Warren felt displaced when his family relocated to Washington, D.C. His grades tanked and his good habits gave way to bad ones. He would bounce from the University of Pennsylvania to the University of Nebraska, and after failing to gain admittance to Harvard Business School, he ultimately ended up at Columbia, because Benjamin Graham, an economist and author he liked, taught there. It was at Columbia that Warren's love for the stock market grew. He learned everything there was to know about the market and its value in economics.

Warren began by purchasing stock in a small textile company. When prompted to sell the stock back to the company, the owner tried to give him a return that was just slightly off—by just a few cents, in fact. Normally, this would not be a big issue, but for some reason this upset Warren enough that he bought a majority share of the company's stock, fired the owner, and took complete control of the textile business. Warren then used the name of this company to create his umbrella holding firm: Berkshire Hathaway. It was a strange move; however, it speaks to his honest principles: even a few cents off is still not honest business. This was the beginning of his legacy as someone who does things right or not at all.

After years of acquiring controlling amounts of stock in various companies that he liked, Warren came to understand it was best that his corporation never interrupted the daily operations of the companies he controlled. He played the game as a chairman, not a helicopter parent, and this would prove an ingenious way of managing his relationships. Instead of going in and trying to do everything himself, he bought controlling stock in businesses he believed in, run by people he trusted.

Warren Buffett's actions spoke—and speak—louder than his words. In 1990, Salomon Brothers, a large brokerage company that had been submitting false bids to purchase more Treasury bonds, was caught red-handed. When the U.S. Treasury revoked its license, the firm was on the brink of having to declare bankruptcy. Warren, who had no knowledge of these dealings and had even written letters to the company warning against such behaviors, stood up and took the blame. And this was a time, not unlike today, when many CEOs preferred hiding behind curtains of secrecy. Buffett, on the other hand, knew that if the company sustained that loss, not only would the Berkshire stockholders take the hit, but also eight thousand jobs would be lost. At a board of directors meeting, he took the position of interim chairman and convinced the U.S. Treasury that practices such as these would never occur again under his jurisdiction. Read that again. He stood up, apologized for someone else's mistake, and simply *promised the government that it wouldn't happen under his watch.*

This move demonstrates the power of a persona as a public brand, managed properly: Buffett's name had become so synonymous with honesty, integrity, insurance, success, and good judgment that the Treasury eventually released its hold on the company's license *on his word*. This sort of movie-magic moment seems mythical and impossible to obtain, but I'm telling you that *you can do this too*—if you never waver from your brand and what you stand for, and if you say what you mean and mean what you say. Life is like an ad campaign: the more consistently you stay *on message,* the more people you will convince. Did Warren have a hand in the wrongdoing? No. But he cared about the ultimate consequences of remaining silent. A man as handy with math as Warren Buffett knew that those eight thousand lost jobs would affect more than just those eight thousand lives; the cumulative result would effectively damage the market, ruining countless more lives. To take a personal blow like this and remain resilient is a source of real power and only bolsters his image as utterly *trustworthy*. This honesty is his brand, his personal "stock," beyond his billions—and a major source of his power. People buy stock in Berkshire because they are buying Buffett himself—they want a piece of his brand that he protects so staunchly.

Warren would go on to become the richest man in the world, year after year, until he was eventually surpassed by Bill Gates, with whom he developed a deep relationship and a friendly rivalry. So what do you do once you've achieved more money and power than arguably anyone else in the world? Well, Warren decided to pledge more than half of his fortune—$37 billion—to the Bill and Melinda Gates Foundation, one of the largest single donations to charity in history. To this day, his contributions (which add up to around $2 billion so far, with more pledged after his passing) have been used in countless ways to help fight disease and wealth inequality, to bolster public education programs, to develop new technologies . . . the list goes on.

When I say that the end justifies the means, when I tell you to be ruthless in achieving your goals and to put on your oxygen mask first, this is why. Buffett is able to improve the lives of countless people, including but not limited to the people who work for the companies he owns, because he achieved power first.

If you climb the mountain first, you can let down a ladder.

FRANK UNDERWOOD

Power is a lot like real estate. It's all about location, location, location. The closer you are to the source, the higher your property value.
—Frank Underwood

Yes, I know, Frank Underwood is a fictional character, and we already mentioned him when we talked about Machiavelli. But hear me out. For those of you who haven't watched *House of Cards,* Underwood (played by Kevin Spacey) is the fictional main character on the show, and he is a conniving politician who becomes president of the United States in the final season. Since a contemporary pop culture reference can sometimes be more effective than the obligatory classical references, please indulge me an analysis of one scene.

In the opening scene of the very first episode of *House of Cards,* Underwood approaches a dog that's just been involved in a hit-and-run with a car. As Frank looks up from the dying animal, he breaks the fourth wall (as he often does), and as the sounds fade away, he lets the audience in on a little secret: "There are two kinds of pain. The sort of pain that makes you strong or useless pain. The sort of pain that's only suffering. I have no patience for useless things." Then, with cool-headed deliberateness, Frank calmly places a hand around the dog's neck and puts it out of its misery. He continues: "Moments like this require someone who will act, who will do the unpleasant thing, the neces-sary thing." The dog's muffled whimpers cease. Frank looks down and, speaking to the deceased animal, says, "There. No more pain."

This scene vividly illustrates the Machiavellian ar-gument, perhaps even more so than the historical refer-ences and stories we've explored up to this point. As I've stated before, Machiavellianism is not about good versus evil. So set aside questions like: Is it right to kill an innocent dog? Is it wrong to let it suffer? Machiavel-lianism is about the ends, the consequences of actions, and about the will to do what needs to be done. In his book *The Psychopath Inside,* which I read on rec-ommendation from my son, neuroscientist Dr. James Fallon talks about how feeling empathy can help us be-come better people, but in moments of extreme stress, it can inhibit our ability to act promptly. Empathy re-quires us to pass decisions through the orbital cortex and the amygdala, which takes more time and slows down reaction speed. In times of crisis, this is not good for anyone. So call Frank Underwood a psychopath if you must, but according to Dr. Fallon, getting rid of psychopathic behavior entirely is not necessarily the answer, because cold, calculating people are the ones who get the job done. As he explained in a 2014 inter-view with the *Huffington Post:*

> In times of great biological stress, [psychopaths] save the species . . . If you take a look at the development of human cognition, the greatest explosion of brain size occurs during periods of

great climate change . . . Once the environment changes drastically, what's considered moral and normal changes . . . You need that person. When the asteroid hits, there's nobody to take the ball and run with it . . . By opening up normative behaviors (and moral behavior is really just normative behavior; it's the average behavior) psychopaths teach us how much our limbic system and our sense of morality compromise our efficiency.

To continue with the example of Frank Underwood, let's ask ourselves: What would most others have done when facing this situation with a dying animal? They would likely have wasted valuable seconds, maybe minutes, panicking, scrambling around, and lamenting the situation. Maybe, eventually, someone would have rushed the suffering animal to the vet, hopefully without hurting it while lifting it up and loading it into a car, but possibly further traumatizing the animal and themselves. All of this rushed activity would go on while the dog experiences excruciating pain from a broken back, from being carried from ground to car, car to vet bed. In the end, the vet would likely say that there is nothing to be done and that the animal would have to be put down. Sure, there's a chance that the dog could have survived. Maybe. But in this scenario, let's assume that it *would not have survived*. The dog's injuries were too obviously severe. In this case, Frank's behavior seems entirely justified, and the faster he gets it done, the better. What else could have been accomplished, except the prolonged suffering of the animal? Frank Underwood had the cold, calculating calm that was necessary. He wasn't needlessly cruel; he was just able to analyze the situation objectively, without resorting to the flits and flourishes that accompany strong emotion.

That's a power decision. I've had to make plenty of decisions like this in the past, in scenarios that would otherwise make someone panic. I will have to make many more, as will you. The objective is to know how and why you make your decisions, and to have a clear enough head to act decisively and promptly.

Frank Underwood goes on to do some pretty horrific things to other people in *House of Cards,* so one might say he's a terrible example of Machiavellianism as a virtue. As a counterpoint, I would ask: What does Frank Underwood do right? He's great at waiting and striking while the iron is hot. He's sharp with his tongue and appeals to the common man as well as to his fellow members of Congress. His ability to garner power is useful to his own ends. And what if his ends were yours? Wouldn't his tenacity and his strategic thinking (with a few minor adjustments) make him the kind of man you would want on your side?

If you find psychopaths terrifying, it is likely because they are the most *effective* at the evil they do. So I would ask you to seize this power for yourself, to more effectively accomplish your own (virtuous) goals. Be a psychopath with a conscience. Be ruthless, yet loved and law-abiding. Remember: power is inherently neutral. Once you gain it, you will have the freedom to use it for good or for ill.

GO FORTH

I could wax philosophic all day about power, about my heroes, about the people who have influenced me and the things I have accomplished. But the only variable that will make a difference is *you*. As we've discussed, it is not your motivation, or your emotions, or how hard you wish and pray that gets the job done. It is your *actions* and the *consequences* of those actions that matter. Everything else is noise. Hopefully this book will serve as a catalyst for you to get out there and take action.

Get out there and take notes, and plan for your future. Get out there and self-educate. Get out there and find your first job. Work hard enough so that when you ask for a raise at that job, your boss says yes. Then get out there and find a second job. Get out there and decide what you want to do with the rest of your life. Learn from those who are doing what you want to do and become better. Become the product you wish to sell and the person you would want to hire, and then pass those high standards on to those around you. Once you've done that, keep going. Get addicted to it. Work that you are passionate about is the best drug in the world, I assure you. So get to it.

I have run the gauntlet of life, and I am sure as hell not done yet. I have had my share of life lessons, and I keep learning all the time. So should you. I want to make you powerful. Yes, *you*! And why shouldn't you be powerful? We all have dreams. We all want to be *more*. With more power, you could be a job creator, you could give more to charity, and, of course, you would have the power to make sure your family is healthy and happy and protected. Power begets more power, if we create a culture of encouragement instead of one of envy and jealousy. Don't tear others down. Raise yourself higher than them. Love alone, I am sorry to say, cannot do that. At the end of the day, love may be what we stay alive for and thrive on, but we must have *power* to live, before we philosophize about why we're doing it at all.

Power and, yes, *money* will certainly increase your chances of making you, and those around you, healthier and happier.

The world is waiting for you.

Go forth.